WAR IN THE HEBREW BIBLE

WAR
IN THE
HEBREW BIBLE

A Study in the Ethics of Violence

SUSAN NIDITCH

New York   Oxford
OXFORD UNIVERSITY PRESS

Oxford University Press

Oxford New York Toronto
Delhi Bombay Calcutta Madras Karachi
Kuala Lumpur Singapore Hong Kong Tokyo
Nairobi Dar es Salaam Cape Town
Melbourne Aukland Madrid

and associated companies in
Berlin Ibadan

First published in 1993 by Oxford University Press, Inc.
198 Madison Avenue, New York, New York 10016

First issued as an Oxford University Press paperback, 1995.
Oxford is a registered trademark of Oxford University Press, Inc.

Library of Congress Cataloguing-in-Publication Data
Niditch, Susan
War in the Hebrew Bible: a study in the ethics of violence
Susan Niditch.
p. cm. Includes bibliographical references (p.) and index.
ISBN 0-19-507638-9; ISBN 0-19-509840-4 (pbk)
1. War—Biblical teaching
2. Bible. O.T.—Criticism,interpretation, etc.
I. Title
BS119.W2N53 1993 221.8'355—dc20 92-5787

6 8 7 5

Printed in the United States of America
on acid-free paper

For Robert, my dear husband,
on the occasion of our
eighteenth wedding anniversary

ACKNOWLEDGMENTS

This book was written with the generous and much appreciated support of the National Endowment for the Humanities and Amherst College. I thank the many colleagues who read portions of the manuscript or drafts of the whole, providing encouragement and useful insights or who offered valuable bibliographic and methodological suggestions. These include Lawrence A. Babb, Claudia V. Camp, Carole R. Fontaine, JoAnn Hackett, Theodore Hiebert, David Little, Peter Machinist, John P. Reeder, Philip Stern, Gene M. Tucker, David W. Wills, Robert R. Wilson, William F. Zimmerman, and the members of the Colloquium for Biblical Research who met in Rochester, New York in August 1989. Diane Beck graciously prepared the manuscript. I received additional assistance from my students Katherine Davis and Catherine Lhamon.

An earlier draft of chapter 3 and small pieces of the introduction have been published in a volume of Semeia, *War, Woman, and Metaphor*, edited by Claudia V. Camp and Carole Fontaine. I thank Scholars Press for permission to incorporate this material into my book.

Finally I thank my children Rebecca and Elizabeth for their love and their infectious energy, and my husband Robert Doran for all his help with this particular project, but also for being the most supportive and loving friend a wife could have.

CONTENTS

ABBREVIATIONS

ANET	*Ancient Near Eastern Texts*, ed. James B. Pritchard. Princeton: Princeton University, 1950.
ASOR	American Schools of Oriental Research
BA	*Biblical Archaeologist*
BAR	*Biblical Archaeology Review*
BASOR	*Bulletin of the American Schools of Oriental Research*
BDB	F. Brown, S.R. Driver, and C. A. Briggs, *A Hebrew and English Lexicon of the Old Testament*. Oxford: Clarendon, 1968.
bMeg	Babylonian Talmud, Tractate Megillah
BR	*Biblical Review*
bSan	Babylonian Talmud, Tractate Sanhedrin
BZ	*Biblische Zeitschrift*
CBQ	*Catholic Biblical Quarterly*
CBQMS	*Catholic Biblical Quarterly Monograph Series*
HSM	Harvard Semitic Monographs
IB	*The Interpreter's Bible*
IDB	*The Interpreter's Dictionary of the Bible*. New York: Abingdon, 1962.
IEJ	*Israel Exploration Journal*

JAOS	*Journal of the American Oriental Society*
JBL	*Journal of Biblical Literature*
JSOT	*Journal for the Study of the Old Testament*
NEB	The New English Bible
NRSV	New Revised Standard Version of the Bible
RB	*Revue Biblique*
RSV	Revised Standard Version of the Bible
UF	*Ugarit-Forschungen*
VT	*Vetus Testamentum*
ZAW	*Zeitschrift für die alttestamentliche Wissenschaft*

WAR IN THE HEBREW BIBLE

Introduction

A Chain of Tradition: The Terrible Burden

On 1 September 1689 Cotton Mather preached his sermon "Souldiers Counselled and Comforted," a charge to members of the armed forces engaged in the ongoing battles with the native inhabitants of New England. One can imagine oneself a young man preparing to fight those whom the minister calls "Murderers" or picture oneself a mother preparing herself to let the son go to face the "Wolvish Persecutors." The mood is intense, electric with blood-stirring references to beloved friends killed by Indians (Mather:9, 31, 32), to the need for courage, and to the faith owed a supportive but demanding God. The sermon is rich in the words and syntax of the King James version of the Hebrew Scriptures, for these are folk for whom the written Scriptures have been "reoralized." The Bible is alive to the people gathered at the Old North Meeting House, Boston, in the oral formulations of the Puritan preacher who combines traditional phrases and ancient images to describe perceptions of current realities. The cadences of the Bible speak the listeners' myth. They are Israel in the wilderness, confronted by Amalek (Mather:37), Israel who must approach the enemy with a priestly purity of body and soul (Mather:17, 24, 25, 38). Amalek, deserving of vengeance and total destruction, is to be "beat(en) small as the Dust before the Wind," "Cast out as the Dirt in the Streets," (Mather:28) eliminated, exterminated. The war against the Indians of New England is justified on grounds both

3

explicit and implicit: they are accused of murdering Christians and
therefore are worthy of death (so some biblical writers justify killing
in war), but also they are Ammon, Amalek, an indigenous population
who will be displaced and disinherited by divine decision to make way
for the new Israel. Mather is in a lengthy tradition of Christian
preaching on war when he treats the enemy as Amalek and the
fighting as justified crusade. So European Christians were encouraged to join in the crusading wars against the Saracens by religious
leaders quoting Hebrew Scriptures (Bainton:112–33); so British Puritans and non-Puritans before Mather justified war (Bainton:150–51;
Johnson, 1975:98, 111–12, 118–21); so the campaigns against native
Americans were justified well into the eighteenth century as preachers
such as Herbert Gibbs prayed thanking "the mercies of God in
extirpating the enemies of Israel in Canaan." (Bainton:168) This
ongoing identification between contemporary situations and the warring scenes of the Hebrew Bible is a burden the tradition must guiltily
bear. The particular violence of the Hebrew Scriptures has inspired
violence, has served as a model of and model for persecution, subjugation, and extermination for millennia beyond its own reality. This
alone makes study of the war traditions of the Hebrew Scriptures a
critical and important task. The Hebrew Bible, moreover, like any
masterwork of human invention reflects who we are, our very nature
as people. To understand attitudes toward war in the Hebrew Bible is
thus to gain a handle on war in general, the motivations, justifications,
and rationalizations of its wagers, and yet other issues are more culturally and historically bound.

Tracing Roots, Assigning Blame

Mather and the other noteworthy Christians fully believed themselves recipients and continuers of a particular biblical tradition,
but their use of Hebrew Scriptures surely says more about their
own forms of self-articulation than about ancient Israelite attitudes
and traditions. This distinction is not drawn clearly enough by
several modern scholars. It comes as no surprise that modern
students of war trace a trajectory of justified crusade back to the
Hebrew Scriptures. After all, so Bernard of Clairveaux, Mather,
and the others have done. However, they veer strangely off course

when they, like their Christian informants of previous centuries, equate "Israelite" or even more inaccurately "Jewish" views on war with the extirpation ideal. Bainton describes what he calls "the crusading idea" as "originating among the Jews" (Bainton:44) while Johnson declares its manifestation among Puritans as "Hebrew and Jewish." (Johnson, 1975:129–31) Paradoxically, the harsh ideology of the Puritans is somehow blamed on the Jews. It is a short step from these brief assessments to even less nuanced descriptions of other warring threads in the Hebrew Scriptures as reflecting "l'ancien mentalité Juif" (Barucq:130) or proto-Zionist parochialism (B. Anderson, 1954:828). Treatments of a particular ideology of war thus intermingle uncomfortably with generalizations about Jewish world-view, perpetuating the stereotype of the violent "Old" Testament, of law vs. gospel; justice vs. mercy; judgment vs. love.

Another important goal of our study, then, must be to set matters straight, eschewing all-too-easy generalizations about war in the Hebrew Bible, exploring precisely what are Israelite attitudes to war. What Bainton calls the crusading idea in the Hebrew Scriptures is, in fact, not unique to Israelite culture. And within the Hebrew Bible the sort of war of extirpation waged against the Canaanites in Joshua is one among many war ideas as Bainton himself implies (46), a war ideology with which the authors of Chronicles and Jonah, some Deuteronomic threads, and post-biblical authors such as Josephus are uncomfortable. In this monograph we propose to study the range of war ideologies in the Hebrew Bible, seeking to understand who in Israel might have espoused which ideology and when in the history of the biblical tradition. In this way the study of war becomes a study of the social history of Israel, of its complex and variegated culture, as reflected in its rich and wonderfully non-uniform literary traditions.

Previous Work

It is understandable that Bainton and Johnson have not adequately explored the range of war ideologies in the Hebrew Bible. Their interests are, after all, in the subsequent use to which certain threads of the traditions were put. But what of scholars of the Hebrew Scriptures? War, has, in fact, been a neglected topic as

indeed have other areas in the ethics of the Hebrew Bible (noted by
R.R. Wilson:193–95).

Classic works on the ethics of the Hebrew Bible from the early
part of the century generally show little interest in war (Duff).
J.M.P. Smith (129) and Mitchell (173) each include a few descriptive lines concerning Deut 20:10–14 in the context of larger discussions of Israelite attitudes toward foreigners but do not wrestle at
all with troubling dimensions of the ban. One exception is W.S.
Bruce who devotes several pages to the "wars of extermination"
against the Canaanites. He concludes that the total destruction of
Canaanites is justified because they were guilty of "the heinousness
of a sensual idolatry." In this unusual case—not to be taken as a
model for future wars—"moral surgery" was necessary (288–89). "It
was one of those hard necessities to which the God of redemption
condescended." Bruce is, however, embarrassed and concerned
about this particular warring tradition. Managing to weave in a
certain anti-Judaism with his western, Christian bias, he writes,
"Even the Jews have felt as if the command to destroy the Canaanites compromised the gracious character of Jehovah."

Some current works on Old Testament ethics do not discuss war
per se but have other important methodological agendas exploring
more broadly how the Hebrew Bible might inform contemporary
moral decisions (Birch and Rasmussen; see also Childs, 1970:59–60,
123–38, 189–98; and Childs, 1979:82–83 and throughout) or discussing the means by which to evaluate the ancient sources of ethics
in the Hebrew Bible (Barton).

Douglas Knight's brief but seminal article is an especially useful
contribution providing a fine concise working definition of the
areas to be explored by those who study ethics in the Hebrew
Scriptures (56).

> Ethics entails critical reflection on the social dimensions of moral
> behavior, the constitution of meaning by both the individual and
> the group, the identification of values underlying moral action,
> the use of warrants in grounding these values, the operation of
> norms and principles in a changing and diversified world and
> similar issues.

Knight distinguishes between descriptive and normative ethics, the
former being the primary focus of the current study: "One should

take pains to describe and understand the ethics of the ancient document and the people who produced it, before trying to appropriate moral norms and directives of the Bible for today" (56). Finally he describes elements that "converge to make up the descriptive task": moral norms and teachings; socio-historical context; forms of moral discourse; theological warrants for morality; views of moral agency and authority; fundamental values (56–58). The works of Barton and Knight in particular point to threads in our own work, providing guidelines and questions useful in exploring the range of war ideologies reflected in the Hebrew Scriptures and the knotty moral issues raised by biblical portrayals of war.

Walter Kaiser and Henrik van Oyen do include brief sections on war in their larger studies of ethics in the Hebrew Scriptures. Kaiser reviews the way in which the biblical traditions are used by later Christian writers on war (1983:173–76), discusses the justness of wars of defense, and with Craigie (1978:93–112) suggests that in offensive wars, human beings are used as God's instrument of judgment. A number of scholars situate Israelite war in the context of divine judgment as we will see below. Van Oyen seeks to show that the ancient Israelites were essentially peace-loving in spite of violent evidence to the contrary and this way skirts the troubling issues faced more squarely by Norman Gottwald (1964) and Peter Craigie (1978) who devote brief works to Old Testament ethics and war. Johannes Hempel's *Ethos* and his article in the *IDB* are more representative of works in Old Testament ethics, displaying interests in covenant, in the ways in which the Israelite community and individuals defined themselves in relationship to their history, land, and God. The issue of war arises in the context of discussing relationships with foreigners or in terms of forms of vengeance for the covenant broken but neither the burden of later appropriations of Old Testament war models nor an attempt to describe various ancient Israelite attitudes toward war occupies Hempel.

Instead of discussing "the terrible burden" or the range of biblical war ideologies as a reflection of variations in Israelite culture, scholars have tended to be interested(1) in questions of historical reconstruction, e.g. did a certain battle take place? Is Joshua's account of Israel's conquest of Israel at all accurate? (e.g. Kang:133–39, 143–44, 146–49, 158–64); (2) in questions of weaponry, the composition of the military, and other nuts-and-bolts logistics of war in ancient Israel (Hobbs; Yadin); (3) in the Yahweh war or holy war which is said to be characterized by certain preparatory acts and rules of purity, priestly roles, and above all the participation of God, "the divine warrior," or his armies (e.g. von Rad, 1953:45–59; 1991; Toombs:787–98; de Vaux, 1961b:258–67; P.D. Miller, 1975; Kang); (4) in the relationships or similarities between Israelite war portrayals and those of non-Israelite ancient Near Eastern materials (Weippert:460–93; Schwally; Malamat, 1966; Schmid; Stieglecker, 1950a:24–27; 1950b:106, 112; Kang).

Introductions to Old Testament life, history, literature, and theology provide surprisingly little description or evaluation of significant variations in war ideology and even less engagement with the ethical dimensions of various forms of war in the Hebrew Bible (Fohrer, 1968; Rendtorff; W. Kaiser, 1975; Noth, 1966; Westermann, 1982). Especially neglected are discussions of the ban, the war demanded by God always including the annihilation of men, women, and children, other times including also the killing of domestic animals, the wanton destruction of whole cities, and the reduction of all cultural artifacts to rubble. Roland de Vaux (1961b) does devote two chapters to describing war in the Hebrew Scriptures, contrasting the banning wars of annihilation in Joshua with the wars in which booty and prisoners are taken during the reigns of the kings described in 2 Samuel and 1 and 2 Kings, and suggests that over time "war became, of necessity, the state's concern; it was 'profaned'" (1961b:263; see also Abel:324–25). Pedersen also provides an interesting full chapter on war and is among those who suggest that the ban with its extreme jingoism appealed to Israelites during periods of particular threat to cultural identity or political survival from within or without Israel (Vols. 3–4:1–32; esp. 26, 27, 31). Neither de Vaux nor Pedersen discusses war in terms of Knight's concern with the social dimensions of moral behavior and questions of values. It is a measure of some scholars' refusal to deal with life-and-death issues raised by the war texts of the Hebrew Bible when van Oyen suggests that the wars of extermination become milder through time because in some texts only humans are killed while the cattle are spared (184)! T.R. Hobbs in a full-length monograph attempts to show how changes in Israelite social structure involved changes in the nature of war, but when he comes to issues of ethics—e.g. why is it permissible to kill suckling babes under the ban—he falls back on the suggestion that these primitive Israelites simply are not like us, their culture is not our culture, their ethics not ours (Hobbs:17, 211). (So too B.W. Anderson, 1957:128, Lasor et al.:207-9.) He goes so far as to suggest that war, in general, was not a problem to ancient Israelites, but was merely accepted as a fact of life. (See also Stieglecker, 1950a:28; Seabury and Codevilla:7-8.)

Other scholars find a home for the ban in the biblical theology of divine judgment (Good:385-400; Eichrodt, 1961:140; Craigie, 1978:74; G.E. Wright, 1969:129-37). Peter Craigie, whose brief monograph like that of Hobbs is among the few devoted to war in the Hebrew Bible, takes the position that war is an evil human activity through which God may work out his purposes of judgment and redemption (Craigie, 1978:54; see also 63, 74). The total destruction of the ban terrible though it is may be legitimate when undertaken to fulfill divine will or to eliminate the greater evil (Craigie, 1978:74). (See also Junker:77, 82; G.E. Wright, 1969:129-31.)

Paul Hanson's brief but thoughtful essay begins promisingly by reflecting upon the difficulty of making sense of the ban tradition for an undergraduate audience. Hanson rejects many of the explanations of the ban outlined above, e.g. it is a war ethic reflecting the "primitive" nature of the Israelites; it belongs to an Israelite theology of divine judgment (33-35). Ultimately, however, instead of grappling with problems in the ethics of war faced by his students, Hanson turns their attention away from the ban itself to emphasize other important and more appealing biblical themes of liberation from oppression and creation from chaos (35-40). Wars must be evaluated in terms of whether they bring about the justice, compassion, and liberation that constitute the true shalom (40). This approach is all well and good, but Hanson goes on to blame all "bad" war material in the Hebrew Bible, such as the ban, on the Israelite monarchy that shaped the stories of the conquest "to give expression to a triumphant royal ideology" (44). This treatment of the "crusading mentality" in the Hebrew Scriptures is too neat and too convenient a way of isolating extremist Israelite war ideologies. The ban in its ferocity cannot simply be rejected as a later accretion or as an untrue reflection of the real religion of Israel.

In Chapter 1 we will discuss forms of the ban and scholarly treatments of them, exploring synchronically their place in a particular Israelite symbol system and diachronically their place in Israelite social and cultural history. Throughout, however, this study takes the position that the various war ideologies in the Hebrew Bible are equally valid expressions of Israelite culture in its great variety and that Israelites, different though they were from us, did indeed worry about the ethics of war and specifically about the justness of the ban. Their searchings of heart are reflected in narrative traditions of the Hebrew Scriptures and in the confusion and self-contradiction implicit in portrayals of war, from text to text and within texts, as biblical writers themselves attempt to make sense of this violent life-taking phenomenon. We do well to ask first, however, how one approaches the complex texts of the Bible and whose portrayals of war these are.

Methodological Challenges: History and Authors

In recent years, books have appeared with the intriguing titles *Who Wrote the Bible?* (R.E. Friedman, 1987) and *The First Historians* (Halpern, 1988a). Implicit in such titles and the works themselves is the message that scholars pretty much know how the diverse compositions of the Hebrew Scriptures were created, preserved, and put together and that much of the historical-seeming material in the Bible is indeed a record of events, a record preserved from tendentious points of view, but, argues the writer of *The First Historians*, all historiography reflects the vision of its composer (8).

The authors who produced these books are in a long pedigreed scholarly tradition when they write of specific sources or documents behind the Hebrew Bible and when they refer to individuals or schools responsible for preserving or putting together one or another of these documents. I too agree that behind the Bible lie many different sources and that some biblical works evidence astute historiographic consciousness and contain valuable information about real historical events, but I am not nearly as sanguine as some of my colleagues that scholars are able precisely to reconstruct either the literary history of the Hebrew Bible or the history of events to which the Bible often alludes. We know embarrassingly little about the education process in biblical times that might have trained scribes or about bardic traditions that might have produced singers of tales. We are far from certain about matters of literacy or even about the physical means by whch manuscripts might have been preserved (W.V. Harris; Crenshaw, 1985). More often than not we have no extra-biblical evidence corroborating that events related in the Bible, however historiographic the style of the telling, ever occurred. So much of what we do as biblical historians involves "taking things on faith" in more than one sense of the phrase. These basic problems in text and history greatly complicate efforts to understand how biblical texts reflect the lives, experiences, and beliefs of real people set in time and place and emerge with troubling clarity when dealing with the many war texts of the Hebrew Bible as some preliminary examples illustrate.

The first war text of the Hebrew Scriptures, Genesis 14, is the story of Abram's military rescue of his nephew Lot. This passage has baffled generations of scholars and the bibliography concerning it is extensive. Does this text preserve the historical kernel of a real battle? If so, when might the battle have taken place? Who are the protagonists and what causes are at issue? Even if no real battle is the basis of Genesis 14, does the text accurately reflect one author's knowledge of war at a particular period in Israelite history? If so, what does the passage say about the ways in which battle is waged, about the formation of military alliances, fighting forces, the allocation of tribute, and the ways in which contentious issues are resolved? What is the literary form of Genesis 14? Is it to be characterized as epic, legend, folktale, or historiography? Does its author intend to write history? Does the text reveal particular attitudes to war, an ethic of war? To what sort of author might such attitudes belong? Indeed, how many authors or sources may lie behind the narrative now found in the Bible? Questions concerning the literary history and form of Genesis 14 and the possible historical implications of the passage are complex, answers elusive.

But what of non-narrative genres in the Hebrew Bible? Are legal texts less equivocally informative on a basic level of exploring the history of war in Israel? Does Deuteronomy 20, for example, tell us anything about actual rules for engagement in war in some period in ancient Israel? In fact Deut 20:10–18 contains contradictory rules—one allowing the enemy to surrender and be spared, another requiring the total annihilation of the enemy—joined by the statement in v. 15 that the harsh treatment applies to enemies geographically near to Israel, the more lenient treatment to those further away. Yet, the "near" or "far" distinction is very inconsistently applied in other war texts, and appears more an attempt to harmonize contradictory war ideologies than a workable rule of war. And so, legal material presents as many challenges as narrative.

The questions multiply as one moves from Deuteronomy with its own special homiletical style to the many war texts of the so-called Deuteronomistic or Deuteronomic History running from Deuteronomy through 2 Kings. How does one assess the disparate war materials in what most scholars regard as one of the major biblical "sources" or "documents?" Problems in assessing the meanings and messages of war texts within the literary history of the Deuteronomic corpus spill over into vexed historical and sociological questions about the Israelite "conquest" of the land, about the transition to the monarchy, and about the nature of political authority in the days that kings ruled. What is the relevance, moreover, of extra-biblical material such as the Moabite Mesha Inscription to an understanding of the ideology of total destruction found in Deut 20:16–17 and elsewhere in the Deuteronomic History?

The study of war in the Hebrew Bible thus involves confronting fundamental issues in Israelite history and the history of the biblical text, work with an array of literary genres, and the challenge to make sense of divergent views of war held by biblical authors. If, however, the study of war in the Hebrew Bible is a difficult puzzle, it is also a key. If all war texts do not contain verifiable information about particular battles and wars or about the logistics of war in a particular period, all war texts whatever their genre do offer information about their authors' ideologies, world-views, and attitudes. If Genesis 14 does not preserve a record of a battle of Abram or provide a guide to how wars were really fought at some point in the history of ancient Israel, this text does record how its author pictures a battle of Abram, and that image is filled with informative significance for understanding the history of ideas of war in Israelite culture. The patriarch is portrayed as socially equivalent to the warrior kings around him, but a leader who undertakes war only for defensive purposes to right an injustice, and who does not seek to profit from the battle. The author who creates such an image of Abram would presumably believe in the use of military power for moral purposes. This already says a great deal.

Through the study of the large but finite number of biblical texts dealing with war, one, in fact, gains access to a range of other matters central to an understanding of the biblical corpus and the intellectual history of Israel. Attitudes toward war are a cultural map of sorts, war being a world in itself in which relationships between life and death, god and human, one's own group and the other, men and women are put in bold relief. Biblical texts concerning war serve as templates of key belief systems in which views of war go hand-in-hand with attitudes to other major issues theological, ethical, political, and philosophical. In this way, asking who might have accepted one or another ideology of war may provide insight into the various groups that lie behind the Hebrew Scriptures and reveal important keys to biblical authorship. And so, while the methodological challenges described above make our task difficult, the study of war may shed some light on some of the most difficult questions we face in the study of Scripture, questions concerning the variegated traditions that now form the Hebrew Scriptures and concerning the Israelites' own often wrenching efforts to understand and define their cultural identity.

Cross-Disciplinary Approaches to War

To study war in the Hebrew Scriptures is to test one's methodological assumptions as a biblical scholar, but is also to immerse onself in rich and complex debates among ethicists, political scientists, psychologists, anthropologists, biologists, and other students of war. A thorough review of currently available scholarship on war would require a book in itself, but it is possible and helpful to discuss major themes raised by scholars whose approaches suggest other questions of biblical texts than are usual in biblical scholars' treatment of them.

Types of War and Social Organization: Defining Society, the Self, and the Other

A.R. Radcliffe-Brown opens the anthology *African Political Systems* with some important generalizations useful to the student of war in the Hebrew Bible. First, every human society has some sort of political and social organization (1940:xiv) and essential to that organization is the "maintenance or establishment of social order . . . , by the organized exercise of coercive authority through the use, or the possibility of use of physical force" (Radcliffe-Brown, 1940:xiv; see also Q. Wright, 1942:70). To study war or attitudes toward wars (even in texts that may not be records of real wars) is in part to ask what social organization is assumed by the people for whom the text is meaningful and who is envisioned to hold the power to use coercive authority. I use distancing terms such as "is envisioned to" because relationships between war portrayals in biblical literature and ancient Israelite political life are always complex and often elusive. The priestly writer of Numbers 31, for example, imagines an army led by one of his own, that is, by a priest, and a strongly hierarchical citizenry of priests, commanders, soldiers, and non-combatants. This portrayal represents the writer's notion of the way the world should be and presents an ideal order that reflects a particular vision of community, but not the actual way of the world. In fact, the tone and content of this victorious battle report indicate that its author finds his group out of control of its own destiny, politically and militarily. On the other hand, some of the portrayals of war situations in the Hebrew Bible may be linked to the actual exercise of coercive authority by historical figures, reflecting the battles between those who have competing claims to that authority. In this category are events surrounding Saul and Samuel's attempts to deal with the Philistine threat. Saul and Samuel's own battles within the wars against the Philistines have to do with the transition in Israel from a loose tribal confederation led by a charismatic leader to the establishment of a monarchy. The contest between Saul and David in turn underscores the transition from a first tentative experiment with monarchy to the full-fledged dynasty of David, with his permanent capital, his standing army, and his court bureaucracy. Students of war in anthropology and political science, in fact, frequently demarcate between two types of polity and two corresponding sorts of armed conflict, drawing distinctions that may be of relevance to the study of biblical material. As described by Meyer Fortes and E.E. Evans-Pritchard (5) they are

Group A: Societies which have centralized authority, administrative machinery, and judicial institutions—in short a government—and in which cleavages of wealth, privilege, and status correspond to the distribution of power and authority.

Group B: Societies which lack centralized authority, administrative machinery, and judicial institutions—in short which lack government—and in which there are no sharp divisions of rank, status, or wealth.

Similar distinctions are drawn by Service who prefers the more utopian and inclusive designations "egalitarian societies" and "hierarchical societies."

Some scholars draw a very sharp line between warring activities in non-primitive and primitive cultures, between war as an organized constructive activity involving the "systematic pursuit" of political objectives and "fighting" of "a more exotic type" including raids for purposes of head-hunting or to obtain victims for human sacrifice or to steal wives (Malinowski:250) or to use Cohen's more ecologically based distinction, between war "as an expression of intergroup hostility resulting from competition for scarce resources, general scarcity, and lack of third party dispute mediation . . ." versus (war as) "a 'reasonable' alternative for the achievement of governmental ends . . ." (338). Alexander Lesser (94–95) in turn draws a contrast between conflict in primitive stateless societies "in which involvement and motivation is [sic] deeply personal" and those in which conflict is essentially "impersonal," functioning to conquer peoples or territory. (See also Schneider:283–91; Malinowski:258; M. Mead:270; Cohen:338.) Like Lesser, Ferguson (17) notes that the shift from the "kin" to "non-kin" basis of war is an important watershed with far-reaching implications. Ferguson (50) understands Cohen to suggest that the challenge to emerging states is to gain control over personal "ethnic hostilities, the military independence of kin-based groups, and the freedom of individual groups to undertake revenge missions." Cohen's work places in bold relief problems implicit in Judges 19–21 in which the kinship ties of the Benjaminites override the right of an emerging Israelite state to impose justice upon miscreants, and in the case of Abner and Joab (2 Sam 2:12–32; 3:26–30) in which David as king is unable to control the latter's kin-based revenge mission. This is not to imply that Judges 19–21 necessarily describes an actual war, but the narrative rich as the Iliad in traditional literary themes of inhospitality, rape, murder, revenge, and women-stealing gives insight into an author's concerns with the very sorts of problems in political self-definition explored by those who work with contemporary field evidence. While one cannot assert that the battle between Benjamin and Israel took place, one might well hypothesize that the author of Judges 19–21 writes during a time when people are reflecting upon the political implications of a transition from a system based on kinship relationships to one that is not. Of course how Israelite authors define "kinship" in one or another period is an important issue, open to discussion.

In the effort to classify the war texts of the Hebrew Bible (as in describing forms of social structure [see Lemche 1985:124, 198, 207–22]) we are, in fact, best served by thinking less in terms of sharp dichotomies than in terms of various spectrums of warring activities (M.A. Nettleship:86–87; Q. Wright, 1942:372–405; Vayda, 1976:12–35; Chagnon, 1977:113–40). Rather than neatly categorize two types of group conflict of which one is not really "war" but revenge, or raid, or feud, some scholars point to a sliding scale between the forms of conflict. The Hebrew Scriptures offer portrayals of war that might be placed at various points on this sliding scale: The raid in Judges 21:13–14 against Jabesh-Gilead to procure wives for the Benjaminites is at the non-state end of the scale. The highly ritualized charismatically led melée that constitutes the battle for Jericho (Josh 6:4–5) is somewhere in the middle of such a spectrum. From the perspective of biblical literary traditions, this battle account like others in the Hebrew Scriptures (Ex 17:8–16; Josh 8:18–19, 10:12–14; 1 Sam 7:9–11; 2 Chron 20:20–30) is a miracle account: the walls tumble down through no human intervention. From a theological perspective it is an example of holy war with troubling ethical implications—all topics to be discussed later in detail. Nevertheless, Israelites fight an enemy with weapons and inflict annihilating losses in order to seize the territory of others. This is a goal appropriate to a portrayal of state-sponsored war, although the form of the fighting force and the mode of engagement have much in common with simpler types of warfare. Finally many of the wars, defensive and offensive, of the kings from David on are more typical of wars waged in "type A" societies. Standing armies, sometimes augmented by mercenaries, are led by career officers in the pursuit of political goals (e.g. 2 Sam 8; 2 Sam 10:15–19; 12:26–31; 2 Kgs 16:5–9). What is interesting is that the feud between Joab and Abner over personal issues and matters of revenge—that is, conflict more within the purview of "type B" societies—intertwines with state-sponsored war. Thus the "line" or "spectrum" is not evolutionary in a simple sense but rather provides a handle by which we might begin to classify and seek to understand the war portrayals in the Bible. Nor is the type of war portrayal found in a text a simple way to date it. We assume, for example, that the book of Judges was preserved by people fully aware of state-sponsored war. Are the descriptions of forms of primitive war in Judges later authors' imaginings of a more tribal phenomenon or does the way fighting is described serve as a marker of genuinely early material that shines through later compositions? These are serious conceptual challenges as we attempt to place the ideologies of the war texts within the history and sociology of Israel.

Another sort of spectrum useful to consider when exploring war in the Hebrew Bible involves the stages of conflict that characterize warring activities in a particular culture. Conflict may begin, for example, on a limited scale and involve relations between a few members of a group and then escalate to another sort of fighting (Vayda, 1976:12–35; Chagnon, 1977:113–40). That is, what begins as a feud between individual members of two in-marrying groups may escalate to small raids and then to full-scale war. The grievous injustice done by criminals in Gibeah of Benjamin to the wife of the traveling Levite in Judges 19 thus escalates to a full-scale civil war between Israel and Benjamin.

A third spectrum involves the way a group defines itself over against other groups, and differences in the sort of warring activity considered appropriate. For example, the pattern of relationships might be as follows: one's immediate family; the kin of one's own patriarchal clan; one's affines, those of one's tribe with whom one marries, but who are not of one's own clan; more distantly related tribesmen; those not of one's tribe. Forms of conflict can be seen as a socio-structural map of sorts reflecting these borders of relationship (Marett:48–67; Sahlins:19). To cite some examples from anthropologists: "Fighting between other Talis clans is not regarded as 'war'; war is the sort of fighting done with traditional enemies who are not Talis clans" (Fortes:245). Within their tribe, the Jibaros of Eastern Ecuador never take heads or engage in raids that result in the total annihilation of the enemy but beyond their tribe do undertake "wars of extermination" (Karsten:313, 316, 322). The Bantu of Kavirondo adhere to "some sort of code" when they fight other Bantu, but not when they fight non-Bantu (Wager:228). Max Gluckman provides a particularly good description of what is allowable in war between Nuer men of the same village, of different villages, etc. all the way to war with foreign people with whom fighting can involve the killing of women and children and the destruction of precious food supplies (8–9). (See also Evans-Pritchard:151–52; E.O. Wilson:109; Radcliffe-Brown:xx.)

Can the war portrayals of the Hebrew Scriptures lead to one or more such socio-structural maps? The question is an extremely difficult one that raises the ever present problem for biblical scholarship concerning the link between the literary and the socio-historical and that underscores our ignorance concerning the sociology of ancient Israel. What does "kinship relationship" mean in one or another period in ancient Israel? What was Israel's tribal structure in pre-monarchic times? These are huge questions that have been examined over the last decade in creative and innovative ways.

Scholars, in particular, have discussed the possible implications of designations in the Bible that appear to classify socio-structural groups: *bêt 'ab* literally "father's household"; *mišpāḥāh*, literally "family," a term that has been taken as a designation for a larger grouping, a clan or lineage; *maṭṭeh* or *šēbet*, an apparently wider grouping, the "tribe." The implications of these terms for understanding Israelite social structure in one or another period have been variously interpreted as scholars debate whether they point to precise or neatly decipherable levels of society (Lemche, 1985:345–90; 1988:91–92; Gottwald, 1979:257–92; Frick, 1979; de Geus:130–50; Pedersen, Vol. 1, 1926:46–60). T.R. Hobbs, in fact, employs Norman Gottwald's analysis of these terms and the conclusions he draws about society in the pre-monarchic period to explain what Hobbs understands to be features of warfare in the period of the Judges. The work of scholars attempting to reconstruct pictures of Israelite social structure on the basis of biblical and archaeological information is worth keeping in mind. War text to war text, we will see if who is portrayed to fight whom and how they fight relates to sociological matters. The battle between Benjamin and Israel (Judges 19-21) and between Samson and the Timnites (Judges 14-15) might be fruitful texts for exploration, for example, since they have to do in part with matters of endogamy, exogamy, kinship, and affinity, key socio-structural issues. Detailed socio-structural maps of the kind charted by modern ethnographers are probably out of our reach, for the Hebrew Bible reflects millennia of cultural development as a corpus of traditional literature revised and revivified by generations of Israelites and as the product of a culture that was never monolithic, even at any one period of time. The war texts of the Hebrew Bible may never provide the sort of detail about tribal relations or relations between villages revealed by actual war behavior among the Nuer that informs the work of Gluckman and Evans-Pritchard. Biblical portrayals of war always, however, reveal much about their authors' concepts of Israelite and other, about these broad and important but shifting categories of the sociological map.

Certain texts such as Judges 8:19 ["If you had let them (my brothers) live, I would not kill you."] imply special kinship concerns in the execution of vengeance and the prosecution of war, as mentioned above, while other texts such as 2 Chron 28:8-11 imply that for some in the tradition the notion of kin has come to include all Israelites. "Send back the captives whom you have taken from your kin" (2 Chron 28:11). It is interesting in this context, for example, that Esau and Jacob and Joseph and his brothers are shown ultimately to reconcile their differences and put rivalry aside, in contrast to the usual pattern of traditional tales of sibling rivalry (see Niditch, 1987:76). The message of these Israelite authors is one of unity among those regarded as descending from Isaac and Jacob in spite of the many differences and rivalries that existed between northern and southern tribes claiming descent from Joseph and his brothers and between Israelites and Edomites, who are said to descend from Esau. Other biblical authors, of course, express much more negative attitudes toward Edom and the northern tribes. Other biblical authors, indeed, define the true Israel much more narrowly than the traditions of Genesis, which brings us to an interesting contrast between the ethnographic evidence presented by anthropologists and the war portrayals of the Hebrew Scriptures. Anthropological evidence suggests that limitations on war appear to be more and more strict, the closer the relationship between the combatants. In the war texts of the Hebrew Scriptures, however, the most unlimited and most annihilating form of war in the spectrum of the Hebrew Scriptures, the ban, is directed not only against foreigners, but also against other Israelites who are accused of straying from God's command. The ban against wayward Israelite cities in Deuteronomy 13 involves the killing of men, women, children, infants and the utter annihilation of all that had belonged to them. So Achan who had kept forbidden things devoted to God for himself after the battle of Jericho is stoned and burned along with his family (Josh 7:24–25). All animate and inanimate things that had belonged to him are destroyed in the pyre.

The ban always involves killing all humans. In no implementation of the ban against foreigners is the destruction of booty quite as complete as in anti-Israelite cases. We will discuss the ban and these most extreme or purist versions of it in chapter 2. We note here, however, that in one thread, at least, of the Hebrew Scriptures, the most complete destruction is reserved for those whom one scholar has named the "indigenous other" (Stulman). Israelites are, of course, not the first or only people to turn upon themselves, to turn their own brethren into the other who is worthy of annihilation, but one of the matters we will want to explore is when and why such breakdowns in group unity occur and who in Israel might consider it appropriate to place other Israelites under the ban. These are matters that begin to raise larger questions in sociology, anthropology, psychology, and biology concerning the roots of war.

Roots of War: Justifying Killing, Underlying Causes

While some maintain that "war is removed from hate and relatively free from guilt" (Wallace, 1967:178), most scholars of war agree that it is extremely difficult psychologically for a human to kill another and that killing and placing oneself in the position of being killed require considerable self-justification, rationalization, psychological and social sanction (Q. Wright, 1942:92–93; 1288–89). And even so, rituals in primitive cultures marking the exit from war frequently emphasize not the jubilance of victory but guilt and ambivalence over those one has killed (Eibl-Eibesfeldt: 191–93). It is even more difficult to kill those "of the group" than those outside the group—hence the sort of map of warring behavior described above. To kill within the group, one must work very hard to dehumanize, to turn one's own people into the other, to delineate between "us" and "them." One of the areas we will want to explore is how Israelite authors describing or discussing war justify the killing and characterize the enemy, internal and external. We hope to show that ancient Israelite writers do worry about the ethics of killing in war and make peace with themselves in various ways. It is a short step from an assertion that killing in war is difficult for people to the question concerning why people allow themselves to do it at all, why all cultures do engage in conflict to the death. What are the roots of war and how do the discussions of scholars in various disciplines concerning the psychological, social, and ecological basis for human group conflict help us to ask new questions of biblical texts?

Few scholars nowadays take the simplistic innatalist position, that war is inevitable because humans are by nature the most violent and aggressive species on earth, instead agreeing that while humans like many other species are capable of tremendous aggression—this trait like our more cooperative side being rooted in the very history of our biological evolution (Holloway:47)—"the capacity for collective violence does not explain the occurrence of war" (Ferguson:8–12; see also E.O. Wilson:101). Many other social, psychological, economic, political, and ecological factors are involved.

One broad area of agreement in exploring factors that tend to encourage war involves group stability and sense of identity. The more stable a group or person is, the surer they are of their identity, the less likely they are to be warlike, and the less rigid and totalistic their war ideologies are likely to be (Jacobs:29–41; esp. 36, 38; G.H. Mead:405; Walsh and Scandalis:141; Eibl-Eibesfeldt:236; see also Carpenter:54 for parallels among non-human species). This is an especially important factor to keep in mind in exploring the spectrum of war ideologies in the Hebrew Scriptures. One would expect to find the ban ideology especially as directed against other Israelites among those who regard themselves as beset, those in a situation of political transition or economic deprivation, ecological scarcity, cultural anomie, or some combination of these. These, of course, are the conditions that give rise to accusations of witchcraft or to the rise of millenarian movements as explored by Wallace (1956), Burridge, Cohn, Middleton, and others. These are also conditions that give rise to war. Paradoxically, the war may lead to a new stability by increasing group solidarity among those who unite against "the enemy" or by actually ameliorating the situation of scarcity or persecution or anomie that may have contributed to instability.

Much of the anthropological work on the causes of war in recent years comes under the heading of "ecological materialism" and we should take a moment to explore this theoretical approach and its relevance to our work. Ferguson provides a balanced and succinct definition of the ecological materialist approach to war (2). "(T)he occurrence and form of warfare are intimately related to processes of material production and other exigencies of survival. The study of war requires attention to human interaction with the natural environment, to economic organization, and to the social, political, and military correlates of both."

Essentially Marxian, this perspective suggests that the root cause of war has to do with basic needs for survival or as Maurice R. Davie put it in 1929 (12) "It is . . . the competition of life which makes war"—competition for land, food, for the means to survive and prosper. It is easy to reduce ecological materialist works on war and other aspects of tribal life to simplistic sounding reductionism. That is, Marvin Harris might be accused of arguing that the origins of war are to be found in the need to control population size to suit available protein resources (1977:36; for somewhat more nuance see Harris 1974:68–69; 1979:90–92; see also Rappaport, 1968:114–17). Napoleon Chagnon's explanation of the constant state of conflict among the Yanomamö has been described monolithically by friends and critics as war to take land (Eibl-Eibesfeldt:182–83 on Chagnon) or war to take women (E.O. Wilson:115 on Chagnon). In fact, many of the scholars who take ecologically based positions (Chagnon, 1967:113; 130–41; Vayda, 1976:2–3; Ferguson:32) are usually more nuanced and complicated in their work. Although scarcity of resources or the need to balance and control resources figure centrally—indeed predominantly—in their explanations of group conflict, they acknowledge the importance of other cultural and political factors. As a scholar of religion concerned with the relation between world-view, ethos, and symbol systems one does wince at phrases such as "the ecosystemic regulatory functions of the ritual cycles (of the Maring) were mystified by its sacred aspects . . ." (Rappaport, 1979:47). Such language portrays religion as the window dressing or perhaps the mask placed upon the "real" materialist functions of ritual and, we might add, of war. In fact, Irenaus Eibl-Eibesfeldt turns to Deut 20:16–17 and Josh 6:21 in the context of the materialist claim that war is often fought for hunting grounds, pasture land, and arable land (185). He states "The Biblical Lawgiver" realizes that "his people needed their neighbors' land as a settlement area. Since men normally have strong inhibitions against aggression directed at women and children, this massacre dictated by cold utilitarian considerations had to be represented as divine command." Even setting aside Eibl-Eibesfeldt's naive assumptions regarding the historicity of biblical texts, one is struck by the simplistic quality of his approach. And yet one should not be utterly dismissive.

Ecological materialist questions may enrich the study of one or another biblical war text. It is, after all, an important and central question to ask whether or not Israelites set out to conquer territory in the second millennium BCE and if some of the war texts are related to conquests in a real historical sense. If not historical in this sense do not the texts about a conquest at least point to authors who feel they must justify claims to certain territory or who feel in less than secure possession of it? Ecological perspectives may also be revealing in assessing differences in the ideologies of war reflected in war portrayals. How does one explain, for example, the requirement of the ban or *ḥērem* that all conquered human beings be killed, contrasted with the taking of young virgin girls in Numbers 31, and with the seemingly more pragmatic taking of male and female war captives elsewhere in the Hebrew Scriptures? The Bible offers its own explanations from passage to passage (e.g. Deut 20:15 discussed above; Num 31:16–17). Do the contrasts in the treatment of enemy captives reflect the perspectives of groups who are or are not able to absorb, feed, and put to work new people, whether as slaves or wives or adopted children (Vayda, 1968:281–82)?

War, Guilt, and Scapegoats

In discussing the roots of war and human beings' reflections upon killing in war, the seminal contributions of René Girard and Walter Burkert should be taken into consideration. Girard and Burkert seek to explain the "formative antecedents" (Burkert, 1987:212) of central aspects of human culture, which they perceive to be rooted in the act of killing, an act that is later ritualized, sacralized, and repeated. For Burkert, the formative "dark event" (Burkert's comments in Hammerton-Kelly:120) is set in the hunt for animal meat. Burkert suggests that the drive to obtain meat in order to live is a basic and fundamental aspect of primitive humankind's emergence as a species, a view for which he has been strongly criticized [see Burkert's own comments (1987:167) and Jonathan Z. Smith's cogent critique (Hammerton-Kelly, 179, 202-5)]. Humans, he suggests, suffer shock and guilt from shedding the blood of living beings (Burkert, 1983:15-19, 21). This guilt is resolved by the ritualization of the kill.

Girard's thesis suggests that the fundamental founding myth of human civilization is not grounded in the theme of breaching divine territoriality, played out in a narrative pattern of interdiction and disobedience as found in the tale of Adam and Eve (Genesis 3) but in the theme of "mimetic violence" played out in the fratricidal pattern found in the tale of Cain and Abel (Genesis 4). Girard writes that humans by their very nature desire to be like those they admire. The need to imitate entails desiring that which belongs to the other. This rivalry results in killing the other to obtain what is his or to supplant him. The victim's relatives in turn kill the killer in vengeance, whose relatives then must take vengenace for him—all of which paints a chaotic and ceaselessly violent picture of what it is to be human. Girard suggests that, subconsciously, in order to break this cycle of deadly violence, the first humans found the alternative of scapegoating. (Girard; 1987:121-29) He writes "men can never share peacefully the object they desire, but can share hatred." The scapegoated victim destroyed by collective violence provides the outlet for and the escape from mimetically induced perpetual violence (1987:128).

Both Girard and Burkert employ the singular language of "original scene" (Burkert, 1987:163), "original act" (Girard, 1977:113), and "original event" (Girard, 1977:276), implying that there was one "dark event" when humans first came to terms with the horror and the implications of their own violence. In recent comments, they appear to nuance this singular language, implying that such encounters with killing (plural) characterize the early emergence period of the human species. These are formative encounters to which, in Eliade's terms, humans must perpetually return and with which they must continue to come to terms. (Burkert's comments in Hammerton-Kelly:212; those of Girard in Hammerton-Kelly:121).

I share much of Jonathan Z. Smith and others' skepticism concerning some of Girard and Burkert's assumptions, such as the former's belief that humans are inevitably "unyielding in their rivalries" (Girard, 1987:125) and the latter's conviction that humans are preeminent meat-eaters (Burkert, 1987:165). Their all-encompassing theories of human origins in violence are magisterial but difficult to accept. Extremely relevant, however, to an understanding of some of the war ideologies of the Hebrew Bible are their emphases on the subconscious guilt that killing can induce and on the human need to sacralize or otherwise rationalize the killing. The war ideologies of the Hebrew Scriptures deal with the guilt in various ways—indeed some trajectories appear to deny it altogether—but much of the large biblical corpus of war portrayals has to do with making sense of the killing, consciously or unconsciously.

Girard's theories of scapegoating, moreover, seem especially relevant to an ideology of the ban in which the enemy is portrayed as the poisonous, sinful, and contagious other who must be cut off in order that the author's community survive. (For a more limited but interesting approach to scapegoating see Maccoby.)

Just Wars and Crusades

Perhaps the most well travelled avenue of inquiry in the western philosophical and scholarly traditions concerning war involves questions about just war. (See reviews by Stout; Johnson, 1991.) While recent scholarship has taken issue with Roland Bainton's work as it applies to the Puritans (Johnson, 1975; Little, 1991), his delineation of pacifistic, just war, and crusading attitudes to war provides useful typologies in exploring the war texts of the Hebrew

Bible. Put simply, wars are entered into justly if the cause is just. Of course, for those who would enter war deciding what is just is no simple matter. Nor is it easy to assess if a group's claims to be engaged in the vindication of justice are valid (Bainton:39). A clear case of self-defense would be just cause to engage in fighting should all other attempts at resolution or mediation fail (Bainton:33). For a large group of biblical writers as well as for later thinkers in the classical and early modern period, belief that God has commanded a war or that God's word needs to be defended are regarded as just causes (Johnson, 1975:9). And so the line between just war and holy war blurs. *Jus in bello*, justness in the fighting itself, has other characteristics, a common one being that the mode of fighting be restrained by a code (Bainton:33). The war "should not be so conducted as to preclude the restoration of an enduring peace" (Bainton:33). Limitations should be set on the prosecution of the war to avoid excessive killing and wanton destruction. The emphasis, then, is on an attempt to limit or restrict the violence of war. Rules for engagement at Deut 20:10-14 that provide the enemy a possibility to surrender and save their lives, rules for sparing fruit trees at Deut 20:19-20, and for dealing with female captives (Deut 21:10-14) all might be seen in terms of a just war code. Of course, enslaving the enemy (Deut 20:11) and forcing its women into marriage are the terms of an oppressive regime and difficult to imagine under the heading of that which is just. These terms certainly would not suit a modern just war doctrine. Such ground-rules do set limits, however; it is in this sense that they are often discussed as a primitive form of the just war (Bainton:43) to be contrasted with the crusade, of which the purest biblical representative might seem to be the ban or ḥērem. Bainton characterizes the crusade as being fought for a divine cause on God's behalf. The line between God's forces and the ungodly enemy is drawn very sharply and the prosecution of the war in Johnson's words is "unsparing" (Bainton:44; Johnson, 1975:137). For an espousal of this sort of ideology we need only turn back to Deut 20:16-18.

> But in the towns of these peoples that the Lord your God is giving
> you as an inheritance, you shall leave nothing that breathes alive.
> You shall surely place them under the ban—the Hittites and the
> Amorites, the Canaanites and the Perizzites, the Hivites and the

Jebusites—as the Lord your God has commanded you, in order that they not teach you to perform all the abominations that they perform for their gods so that you sin against the Lord, your God.

However, as Johnson (1975) finds in Puritan writings, in this particular biblical text a just cause is claimed for the unsparing prosecution (see Deut 20:18). The lines between crusade and just war are thus not at all neat. (See further Walters.) As Michael Walzer says, ". . . the truth is that one of the things most of us want, even in war, is to act or to seem to act morally." (Walzer, 1977:20; see also Q. Wright, 1942:93–94).

In exploring the war texts of the Hebrew Bible we do well to ask about the ways in which biblical writers reveal their own desire "to act or to seem to act morally." What do the war texts reveal about ancient Israelite ethics? Once again we should expect the emergence of a complex spectrum of attitudes, a range of ways in which war is justified, and some disagreement about what is considered allowable behavior in war. Attitudes toward killing and destruction in war, in turn, relate to attitudes toward other aspects of human violence including that fundamental feature of Israelite religion, blood sacrifice.

1

The Ban as God's Portion

The Ban

The most chilling biblical war texts refer to *hērem*, the ban, under which all human beings among the defeated are "devoted to destruction." In one important passage, Num 21:2-3, Israelites vow their enemies to God as a promise for his support of their successful military efforts. In the majority of texts in Deuteronomy and Joshua, it is assumed that God demands total destruction of the enemy. Frequently a reason for the annihilation is provided (e.g. Num 21:23-24; Deut 2:30-35; 7:2-6); in other instances no rationale is provided, only the command or its fulfillment (Josh 6:17, 21; 8:24-29; 10:28, 30, 31-32, 35, 37, 39, 40). Chains of living beings are listed—sometimes including domestic animals but usually not— "man and woman, child and infant, ox and sheep, camel and donkey" (1 Sam 15:3; 22:19); "men, women, and children" (Deut 2:34); "man and woman, young and old, ox, sheep, and donkey" (Josh 6:21). The parallel verbs of destruction help to make the blotting out complete: "strike/devote to destruction/do not spare" (1 Sam 15:3); "we devoted to destruction/we left no survivor" (Deut 2:34); "struck with the edge of the sword/devoted to destruction/ left no survivor" (Josh 10:28). Let no one escape the imposition of total destruction and spare or be spared, a sympathetic mother, a piteous baby. The very language forbids the emotions of mercy. What sort of people might adhere to such an ethic of violence and apparent cruelty? Surely the ban seems counter to fundamental

28

underlying biblical values of the sort that Douglas Knight urges us to uncover: the emphasis on moderation in all things; the importance of preserving life. Warnings against shedding human blood in Gen 9:5, emphasis on care for widows, orphans, and aliens found in Ex 22:21–24 (vv. 20–23 in the Hebrew), the way in which witnesses in capital cases are adjured not to be the cause of an innocent person's death (Deut 19:15–20) all seem to offer an ethic counter to that of the ban. Where does the ban belong in an Israelite symbol system? Is it necessarily incompatible with a life-affirming ethic? How does one explain seeming inconsistencies in descriptions of the ban? How many types of ban ideology are there and how do the various ban texts define Israel and the "other" and for whom? How do we explain ancient and modern writers' treatment of ban traditions?

Several scholars have explored the range of meanings assigned the term *ḥērem* in non-biblical ancient Near Eastern literatures, finding nuances including "to become sacred, inviolable," "to be accursed," "to be consecrated for destruction," and a possible association with burning (Brekelmans, 1959a:17–53; Stern, 1989:1–18; 1991:5–17). The biblical evidence shows a similar range. One fundamental place to start in exploring this most shocking of ancient Hebrew ideologies of war is with the meaning separated, set aside, rendered sacred for the use of God or his priests, for this meaning of the root *ḥrm* links together several biblical non-war and war usages of the term and the Mesha Inscription, a close Near Eastern parallel—all under the heading of sacrifice.

The Ban in a Sacrificial Context

In a non-war context Lev 27:28 states that anything that a man devotes to God (*ḥrm* verb used) from among his possessions—human beings (i.e. slaves), animals, or agricultural holdings—cannot be purchased or redeemed. "Every devoted thing (*ḥērem*) is 'a holy of holies' (*qōdeš qădāšîm*) to God." In a similar vein, Lev 27:21 juxtaposes "holy to God" *qōdeš* with *ḥērem* in reference to a person's pledge of land. That which is *ḥērem* in these contexts is not a destroyed item or person but a possession devoted and sacrificed, given up for the use of God or his priests. (See also Ezek 44:29.) The set-apart *ḥrm* item is thus to be contrasted with that which can be transferred, sold, or redeemed and thereby reintegrated into the human or mundane realm. The terms *ḥrm* and *qdš*, "set apart for God," "holy," contrast with *mkr*, *g'l*, and *pdh*, "sell," "redeem," and "ransom" (e.g. 1 Sam 14:45; Lev 27:29). Yet are human beings whose death is also demanded in other *ḥērem* contexts an acceptable sacrifice to God? Lev 27:29 implies that this is, in fact, the case, for a banned human being destined for *ḥērem* is not to be redeemed/ransomed (*pdh*). "He will surely die." The phrasing of Lev 27:28, concerned with objects and people devoted to God's service, is identical to that of Lev 27:29, which refers not merely to service, but to someone condemned to death under the sacral prescriptions of *ḥērem*.

The *ḥrm* term is also found in an interesting priestly passage that juxtaposes setting aside objects for the use of God and God's priests and matters of sacrifice and redemption. "Every *ḥērem* (devoted thing) in Israel is to be yours," i.e. the priests' (Num 18:14). "The first issue of the womb of all creatures that are offered to God among humans and animals are for you, but you will surely redeem (*pādōh tipdeh*) the first-born of humans . . ." (Num 18:15). The priestly writer responsible for this passage rejects the notion of literally sacrificing first-born humans—the fact that he has to emphasize the point is in itself an interesting comment on the wider world-view of his culture, a matter to which we shall return. In any event, the rhetoric and imagery of Num 18:17 is a reminder that even this priestly writer, with whom we can be comfortable because he exempts humans from sacrifice, regards God as a blood devourer. The animal's blood is dashed on the altar, its fat turned to smoke for the deity's savoring.

Some scholars tend to discount the importance of references to *ḥērem* in Leviticus, Numbers, and Ezekiel, dismissing them as late, "civilized" (Stern, 1989:186; 191:125) versions of whatever *ḥērem* once was in the religion of Israel; "*ḥērem* has been reduced to a technical term" (Stern, 1989:186). (Yet contrast Stern, 1989:198–200; 1991:134–35). The lateness of these texts, however, proves only that the sacrificial nuance of the ban is alive and well in late biblical works as confirmed also by some prophetic, poetic texts discussed below. The concept of *ḥērem* as God's portion is deeply rooted in

Israel, informing both priestly non-military ban texts and the war texts discussed in this chapter.

From people and things devoted to God in a non-war context we turn to the Mesha Inscription and comparable biblical evidence.

> Now Kemosh said to me, "Go seize Nebo from Israel. So I went at night and fought against it from the break of dawn until noon. I seized it and killed everyone of [it] seven thousand native men, foreign men, native women, foreign women, concubines—for I devoted it to 'Ashtar-Kemosh'" (lines 14–17, trans. Jackson, p. 98).

> So I went by night and fought against it from the break of dawn until noon, taking it and slaying all, seven thousand men, boys, women, girls, and maid-servants for I had devoted them to destruction for (the god) Ashtar-Chemosh, (ANET, 321, trans. W.F. Albright).

Touted in the nineteenth century as "the greatest Biblical discovery of modern times," (Graham:42), the Moabite Stone is a victory stele upon which Mesha, the ninth century BCE king of Moab, describes his victory over Israel. The Mesha Inscription (MI) provides fascinating insight into the religion, history, and war ideology of ancient Israel's southeast bordering neighbor, so frequently and disparagingly mentioned in the Hebrew Bible. (For full text and translation see Jackson and Dearman and Jackson.) For Mesha, the Israelite Kingdom under Omri had been the overbearing oppressor (MI, line 5), able to oppress because Chemosh, Mesha's god, had been angry with the land. Now states Mesha, his god has delivered him. Mesha revolts, gains independence for his people, and claims that Israel has "utterly perished forever" (MI, 1.7)—a wishful claim that parallels those of the Israelite writers of the biblical ban texts. Mesha explains further that his god Chemosh had ordered him to capture the city, Nebo, from Israel. The above excerpt is Mesha's description of the battle and its aftermath. The term translated "devote" or "devote to destruction" is the root *ḥrm* found also in the biblical ban texts.

Many scholars have pointed to linguistic and conceptual connections between this war text and various biblical texts in which a war is commanded by the deity and the conquered enemy is annihilated as that which is devoted to the deity (Stern, 1989:19–76; 1991:19–56; Mattingly:214–15; Jackson). One of the closest, simplest biblical parallels to the above excerpt from the Mesha Inscription is offered by Num 21:2–3. Israel confronts the Canaanite enemy, the king of Arad and his forces who have already taken some Israelites captive. Israel makes a vow, the real thrust of which is obscured by the NRSV. Compare the NRSV and then our translation. "Then Israel made a vow to the Lord and said, 'If you will indeed give this people into our hands, then we will utterly destroy their towns.'" Why should such a vow of wanton destruction please the deity? Rather Israel promises something for something, a deal that the deity presumably cannot resist—not wanton, meaningless destruction but an offering for his use and devotion: "If you will indeed give this people into my hands then I will devote their cities to destruction." Israel is promising a sacrifice to God, the cities and their content. So the Moabite king had promised his Israelite enemies to his deity.

Vows to the deity, promises in exchange for divine favors, are common in Israelite war descriptions. So Saul takes an oath, a curse upon himself, that his men will not eat before evening, the time when vows cease to be in force, in order that Saul "might be avenged on (his) enemies." Thus, in the cause of victory Saul takes upon himself and his men a promise of self-denial as an act of devotion (1 Sam 14:24). In an interesting twist, Jonathan, Saul's own son eats some honey, special food, a symbol of the life-force, and is nearly himself destroyed (1 Sam 14:27). Saul inquires of God if he should continue his battle against the Philistines (1 Sam 14:37) but receives no answer, the sign of divine displeasure. Ironically, he insists that even should his own son be guilty of breaking the vow, he will be punished by death. God requires recompense. If God has been denied his due, the short-fall must be replaced, even by a life. Urim and Tummim, oracular devices, are consulted to find out who had poisoned the relationship between God and Israel by taking what had been forbidden by Saul's curse. In a similar way, after the defeat at Ai, lots are cast to uncover Achan's theft of articles devoted to destruction, God's ḥērem.

The oracle dramatically discloses Jonathan's guilt, but the people, like Jonathan himself who had scoffed at his father's curse once he had learned about it (1 Sam 14:28–30), refuse to let the hero die and "ransom" him (14:45). Saul's war vow of self-sacrifice thus is shown almost to lead to the death of his son, but the vow is redeemed. This passage is an interesting one, not only in its relevance for understanding the war vow of devotion but also in that it implies a difference in war ideologies. In contrast to this father, Jonathan does not believe in the war vow—better to rely on oneself and a well-fed army. The people will not let the vow lead to a human death. For them, such vows are and perhaps should be redeemable; Jonathan need not die. A much more consistent ideology of vow-making in war is found in the tale of Jephthah.

At Judges 11:30, about to face the Ammonites in battle, a just cause to be discussed below (Judges 11:12–28), the judge Jephthah "vows a vow to the Lord" (the language of vowing is identical to the vow of *ḥērem* made at Num 21:2–3): *wayyiddar neder lyhwh*. The *ḥērem* term itself is not used. "If you will indeed give the people of Ammon into my hand (again note the syntax shared with Num 21:2–3), then whatever comes from the doors of my household to meet me when I return in peace from the people of Ammon will be for the Lord, and I will offer him/it up as a burnt offering." The Hebrew participle "that which comes/emerges" could refer to an animal or a human. From a literary perspective the uncertainty of the object of devotion creates tension and pathos. The same motif is used in some tellings of the folktale, "Beauty and the Beast."

The beast allows the merchant who has taken his rose to exchange his life, forfeit for the beast's rose, for the first thing he sees upon returning home. Again, the beast requires his due. The offering in each case turns out to be the man's daughter. The neutrality of the narrator in Judges 11:29–40 is fascinating and shocking. Jephthah is aggrieved, but the child must go, for such vows cannot be redeemed. The daughter repeats the grounds of the deal (11:36): victory over the Ammonites in exchange for her life. She, like Beauty, is a virgin at a critical juncture in her development having reached puberty but having been untouched or branded by a man. This valuable human commodity becomes the possession of the supernatural being. It is important to note that the tale of Jephthah's daughter does not necessarily imply that ancient Israelite bandit chiefs regularly promised human sacrifices from their own households in order to obtain victory against enemies any more than the tale of Iphigenia indicates that ancient Greek generals generally sacrificed daughters to make the winds move their vessels.

On the other hand, the Greek and Hebrew tales imply world-views in which deities are pictured as appreciating human sacrifice. The tale of Jephthah's daughter is an important myth in ancient Israelite tradition, one apparently linked with notions of separation and maturation for young girls, a ritual marking of their preparation to leave home and father for the husband-beast to which they are to be offered or exchanged (P.L. Day:60). The theme of "Beauty and the Beast" contains the same nuances. In this particular Israelite tradition, however, the offering is also linked with a war-vow and related therefore to the *ḥērem* tradition. God appreciates humans offered to him.

Specific vow language is not found in the many other *ḥērem* texts located mostly in Deuteronomy and Joshua, but it is in the context of the vow of devotion to destruction, the sacrifice to God, that many of these texts should be understood. In fact, the texts in Deuteronomy and Joshua belong to two trajectories.

In one set of ban texts, reasons and rationales are given for the total destruction. These we will discuss in chapter 2 under "The Ban as God's Justice." One group of biblical writers, like many modern scholars, tries to make sense of the ban in terms of justice in a way that discloses their own discomfort with the sacrifice tradition. But in another set of ban texts, no matters of justice are discussed. The understanding prevails in these texts that God has demanded that all that breathes be devoted to him in destruction. In this category are:

Deut 2:34–35, the defeat of Sihon. Note that all humans are killed—men, women, and children—but that livestock is kept as spoil "for ourselves as well as the booty of the towns we had captured."

Deut 3:6–7, the defeat of Og. Again all humans are killed but livestock and booty are kept.

Josh 6:17–21, the destruction of Jericho in which all living things except Rahab and her family are killed (6:21–22). The town is burned but silver and gold and vessels of bronze and iron are "sacred" (*qōdeš*) to the Lord, going into "treasury of the Lord" (6:19, 24).

Josh 8:2, 24–28, the destruction of Ai in which all humans are killed and the city burned (8:8, 19–20) but spoil and livestock are kept by the people.

Josh 10:28 (concerning Makkedah); 10:29–30 (concerning Libnah); 10:31–32 (concerning Lachish); 10:33 (concerning Gezer); 10:34–35 (Eglon); 10:36–37 (Hebron); 10:38–39 (Debir) and the summary line at 10:40. According to these texts all humans are destroyed; no mention is made of cattle or booty.

Josh 11:11, 14 refers to the death of all humans of Hazor's kingdom; inanimate spoil and livestock are kept as booty.

In all of these passages, the ban involves the killing of all human beings regardless of age, gender, or military status. In Hazor, Jericho, and Ai, the burning of towns is involved, in the case of Jericho, livestock. In most cases, however, booty is kept for the people's own use and towns are not necessarily razed. It is a mistake, in fact, to regard the cases in which booty is said to be taken or cities said to be spared cases of a partial or broken ban. The ban in the texts cited above is properly defined as the devotion of conquered humans to God as in the case of the Mesha Inscription and Num 21:2–3. Only this definition explains the ban's emphasis on killing humans. In giving humans to God, the Israelites are not saving the best booty for themselves. To the contrary, the best sacrifice, the biggest sacrifice, is the human life, as confirmed by the tale of Jephthah's daughter. The Israelites keep only lesser animal and inanimate material for themselves, though even these may in some cases be devoted to God as in the Achan incident.

Perhaps the neatest example of devoting a person to destruction as a sacrifice promised to God is found at 1 Kings 20. The overriding theme of the scene between the prophet and King Ahab at 1 Kings 20 is the issue of God's due, and as in the tale of the forbidden honey, a conflict is described between those who consider the war-vow an integral part of war and those with a more pragmatic view, borne of statescraft. Ben-hadad of Syria has made unjust demands on Ahab that exceed those considered acceptable in the political mores of relationships between dominant and subservient powers

(1 Kgs 20:1–6). War ensues and the Israelites win. Ahab concludes a truce with Ben-Hadad on terms that are extremely beneficial to Israel. Ben-Hadad promises to restore towns his father had taken from the previous Israelite king, and Israel will be allowed to ply trade, setting up bazaars in Damascus. In short, Ben-Hadad gives back territories and opens his markets to Israel. These favorable terms make good sense for Israel from the point of view of statescraft, but a fascinating challenge to the pragmatic ideology of state-sponsored war is found in the dramatic sign act and mashal of 1 Kgs 20:35–38, 39–43.

First, to create his disguise, an anonymous prophet demands that a man strike him and participate in the symbolic scene with him. He refuses and the prophet tells him a lion will kill him (cf. 2 Kgs 2:23–24 and 1 Kgs 13:24). The lion does his work, and when the anonymous prophet asks another man to strike him he does so without hesitation. The wound and bandage provide the prophet/actor with his disguise, but the strike-me scene also relates to the theme of imposing the ban in accordance with God's wishes. He who does not strike when God demands a striking will himself be struck down. It is interesting that in contrast to 1 Sam 15:2–3, a prophet or God himself has not warned the king to place the enemy or enemy king under the ban. The need to devote the enemy king to destruction is understood, a given, in the author's ideology.

In the mashal in 1 Kgs 20:39–43 (cf. woman of Tekoa sent to David at 2 Sam 14:1–20), the prophet weaves a tale for the king. He had been told to guard a prisoner of war. "If he does become missing your life is forfeit for (literally in place of) his or you must pay a talent of silver" (20:39). The prophet goes on to say that the prisoner did escape. Like David in the mashal woven by the prophet Nathan concerning the poor man's lamb, the king condemns the miscreant who is, of course, a symbol of himself. "Thus is your judgment that you have determined." That is, your own words condemn you. The prophet dramatically removes his disguise, the king recognizes him, and then come the words of judgment. "Because you let go the man who was devoted to me (literally "my devoted person"), your life is in place of his and your people are in place of his." No clearer description of the ban as sacrifice exists. The banned king is the Lord's *ḥērem*: if he is found missing, compensation must be provided in the form of the Israelite king's own life.

The ban occurs in Num 21:2-3 and the Mesha Inscription as a solemn promise that human beings will be devoted as a sacrifice to a god in thanks for victory. The ban-as-sacrifice is the ideology behind many of the brief comments on the conquest of cities in Joshua 8 and 10. Humans but not animals or inanimate booty are always devoted under the ban in this context for they are the most valuable offerings. If the vow is reneged upon an equivalent substitute must be found. 1 Kings 20 reveals a tension between this ethic of *ḥērem* as God's sacrifice and the more pragmatic ethic of war as statecraft. Important examples treating the death of enemies as sacrifice and more specifically linking "the ban" and sacrifice are found also in prophetic poetic texts. Some of the following examples have been tossed off by scholars as metaphor (Brekelmans, 1959a:120–21) but such metaphoric texts are rich indicators of their composers' mythology, of shared cultural values and aspects of world-view symbolically represented. Myths and metaphors if properly read may be the truest indicators of essential perceptions of existence.

War, Death, and Sacrificial Feasts

Micah 4:13, a text generally attributed not to the eighth century BCE Judean prophet but to a later post-exilic writer (Mays, 1967:108–9) reveals a prophet's aching for the overthrow of the enemies who have invaded Jerusalem, destroyed the holy temple, and exiled the Judean leadership. In an oracle that begins at v. 11, the prophet poet creates a powerful image of Israel as a strong wild heifer. In the same fashion, many gods, goddesses, and nobility are portrayed in Ugaritic literature as fecund and potent young horned animals. So Yahweh himself is called *'ăbir ya'ăqōb*, a phrase properly translated "the bull of Jacob" (Gen 49:24; Ps 132:2, 5; Isa 49:26; 60:16) (P.D. Miller, 1970). The heifer's horn is to be made of iron, her hooves of bronze. She will crush many peoples and "devote (literally 'I will devote') to destruction for Yahweh their ill-begotten gain/their wealth (or army) to the lord of all the earth." The phrase "devote to destruction for" the deity is evocative of the ban as sacrifice as found in the Moabite Mesha Inscription. Here, however, the offering appears to be inanimate booty, and not humans, which is a significant departure from the most basic root requirements of the ban. The word *ḥyl* does mean army as well as wealth, but the parallel poetry seems to require the inanimate rather than animate meaning. Other late prophetic poetic texts, however, employ *ḥērem* with a very visceral nuance of human sacrifice.

A recurring image in post-exilic prophecy is of the bloody victory banquet to follow Israel's final defeat of her enemies. The motif of the post-victory banquet is a common one in the ancient Near East and indeed in much epic literature that deals with warriors, battle, the heroes' victory. After the ritual preparation for war, the fashioning and bestowing of special weapons, the battle, and the victory, comes a procession, often a palace- or house-building, which in ancient Near Eastern creation texts is synonymous with the defeat of chaos and the creation of the world, and then a celebration banquet in the palace. Exodus 14 and 15 provide images of God's battle with Egypt, the victory, and the people's enthronement (e.g. 15:17); chapters 20–23 outline the law that shapes a world-order; and 24:9–14 briefly alludes to a banquet held in Yahweh's heavenly palace for Moses and the elders of the people. There in a world appearing to be paved with sapphire stone (24:10) they behold God, eat, and drink (24:11). (See also the messianic banquet of Isa 55:1–2.) In the Mesopotamian epic *Enuma elish*, the young god Marduk defeats and kills Tiamat, the mother of the gods perceived as the watery chaos of Sea; he constructs the world from her carcass, ordering it and building Babylon, the dwelling of the gods, and then

> He had the gods, his fathers, sit down to a banquet.
> "Here is Babylon, your favorite dwelling place.
> Make music in [its] place (and) be seated on its square."
> When the great gods had sat down,
> the beer jug they set on, while they were seated at the banquet
> (6:71–75, trans. A. Heidel:49).

Similarly in the Canaanite epic of Baal and Anat, after Baal defeats Yam, Prince River, a male personification of watery chaos, Baal builds his house, and then invites the gods to a feast.

> Baal prepared the house,
> Hadad made preparations within his palace:

he slaughtered oxen,
  he killed sheep,
  bulls, fatling rams,
  yearling calves;
he strangled lambs and kids.
He invited his brothers into his house,
  his cousins within his palace;
  he invited Asherah's seventy sons.
He gave the gods lambs;
  he gave the gods ewes;
  he gave the gods oxen;
  he gave the gods cows;
  he gave the gods seats;
  he gave the gods thrones;
he gave the gods a jar of wine
  he gave the goddesses a cask of wine.
Until the gods had eaten and drunk their fill,
  he gave them suckling to eat,
  with a sharp knife carved the breast of a fatling.
They drank wine from goblets,
  blood of the vine from golden cups

(trans. Coogan: 104).

In late prophetic literature, however, images of the banquet ghoulishly intertwine with images of slaughter in war and blood sacrifice. As Anat plunges knee-deep into the blood of those she has slain in battle (Coogan:90–91) and is satisfied or satiated [the term used is *rwh*, related to one found in the Mesha Inscription (see Stern, 1989:35–36, 284; Albright:279–80), in Jer 46:10, and in Isa 34:5 (see below)], so Yahweh makes a sacrificial feast of the slain. The biblical authors hesitate to suggest that Yahweh consumes the flesh and blood, and various substitutes are found. Thus after the victory over Gog of Magog (Ezek 38–39), a force of evil and chaos in this late-biblical imagining of the final eschatological battle between God's forces and Israel's enemies, it is the birds of prey and the beasts who gather "to eat flesh and drink blood," who drink the blood of the princes of the earth—of rams, of lambs, of goats, and of steers (Ezek 39:17–20). As noted above, in Near Eastern myth these young animals connote princes or nobility (P.D. Miller, 1970). It is thus human young men, killed in war, who are the sacrificial feast, who satisfy (39:13) the appetite of the birds. In Jer 46:10, it is the sword that devours and is sated, drinking its fill of their blood at the Lord's sacrifice. In Isa 34:2-7, the Lord's sacrifice is described in specific banning terms: "He has devoted them (the nations) to destruction, given them over to slaughter. . . . " To whom does Yahweh promise the dead? The poet personifies God's sword as full of blood, gorged with the fat of dead warriors again imaged as lambs, goats, and rams (34:6), wild oxen, steers, and bulls (34:7). Or is it the land that is satiated with blood, the earth gorged with fat? Scholars are certainly correct in suggesting that Isa 34 is metaphoric, the heightened imagery of poetry. The ban is not a clear matter of promise and deal as in Num 21:2-3, but the point needs to be made that deep in the mythological framework of Israelite thought, war, death, sacrifice, the ban, and divine satiation are integrally asociated (Stern, 1989:284; 1991:190-91). To disassociate the Israelite ban from the realm of the sacred and from the concept of sacrifice is to ignore the obvious and yet this is precisely what many scholars have done.

Roots of Discomfort: Interesting Ambivalences

At times the disassociation between the ban and the sacred is an implicit part of the wider critique of von Rad's influential studies, describing the God-commanded, God-led wars of the Hebrew Scriptures as "Holy War" and "a cultic institution." Von Rad's typology of the holy war includes motifs of trumpet blast, consecration of soldiers, proclamation of victory promise by god, Yahweh's leadership, requirement of total belief by Israelites, the enemy's loss of courage due to the "divine terror" that overtakes them, the enactment of *ḥērem* or the ban after the victory, and dismissal of the militia (1991:41-51). (For other treatments of holy war/Yahweh war see Toombs 787-98; de Vaux 1961b:258-67; Smend; P.D. Miller; and the review in Lind, 1980:32-34; for a review of critiques of von Rad's theory see Jones; Ollenburger:22-33). Critiques of von Rad's work emphasize that his neat typology of the holy war is a construct, an idealization derived from many different biblical texts, a product of von Rad's capacity to synthesize rather than an accurate reflection of Israelite culture.

Peter C. Craigie (1978:49) is comforted by these studies asking "Can the ruthless requirement for the extermination of the enemy—men, women, and children—in any way be regarded as holy?" He answers, "I think not. . . . While war was religious by association, it was no more a cultic and holy act than was sheep shearing." More specifically and less emotionally, Walther Eichrodt concludes that the ban in war "cannot . . . be explained either as a sacrificial or as an oblatory act," for human beings are killed, not burned, and the occasional description of the *ḥērem* as *kālîl* (a whole burnt offering) are "metaphoric" (129). Again a belittling by accusation of metaphor. Why would the writer of Deuteronomy 13 choose this particularly visceral metaphor?

One cannot but conclude that many scholars are simply incapable of seeing their God as one who demands and receives humans in exchange for victory, because of world-views shaped by the normative theological expectations of their own religious traditions (Oden). C.H.W. Brekelmans, for example, does suggest that the war *ḥērem* was invoked in earliest Israelite times in particularly critical battles as a means of obtaining God's help (1959a:160–61). Having gone this far in presenting his own interpretation of the ban as sacrifice, he carefully attempts to limit the significance of the phenomenon for an understanding of the Israelite world-view. He allows that only three biblical texts reveal this ideology (Num 21:1–3; Josh 6–7; 1 Samuel 15) (1959a:153; 86–92; 92–98; 106–114) and suggests that the invocation of the war-vow ban came from military leaders or prophets and not from God (179–181; 190). (See the reviews by Weisengoff:443–44; and de Vaux, 1961a:294–95 who points to the theological difficulties in this interpretation.) Like the Rabbis (see below *Tanhuma*, ed. Buber *Wa-Yera* 50, cited in Spiegel: 79–80) he tries essentially to take God off the hook, and in doing so reveals his own discomfort with the tradition, completely skirting fundamental questions about ancient Israelite world-view. He never wrestles with the essential point that some Israelites thought that God desired human beings as offerings (1959a:148–49).

Philip Stern's recent study does view the ban in sacred terms. He comes close to speaking of the ban in sacrificial terms when describing it as "a cosmic act designed to win the god's aid in the battle against the encroachment of chaos" (1989:68; see also 87, 200, 322;

1991:50). But he backs off, emphasizing almost in a materialist way
that the *ḥērem* is a means of restoring "ordered existence" and of
obtaining land (1989:67; 1991:49), all of which helps to restore "the
moral order of the universe" (1989:48, 68). Like Eichrodt, he attempts to compare biblical descriptions of the ban with detailed
prescriptions for certain kinds of sacrifice found in priestly material
and then is able to conclude that the act of *ḥērem* is not imagined by
Israelites to be a sacrificial act (1989:50, 122, 160–61; 1991:107).
There is, however, truly a difference between a detailed priestly
description of ritual and the larger concept of sacrifice implicit in
the ban. The latter is not the purview of ritual professionals, but is a
culturally pervasive notion of what soldiers are doing in vowing to
eliminate all of the enemy or to kill certain individuals in exchange
for victory in war. They are offering human sacrifices to the deity.
The enemy is usually imagined to be slaughtered by sword in the
denouement of battle and not prepared Aztec-style for a separate
sacrifical ritual (See Aho:41–59). Nevertheless, the deaths are perceived as sacrifices to God in exchange for his help in war. This is
recognized by some authors of introductions to the Hebrew Bible.
Carmody et al. write, "people and booty conquered are to be
destroyed, they are the portion of the chief warrior, the Lord"
(Carmody et al:121; see also 104, 127). B.W. Anderson describes
ḥērem as "devoted to Yahweh as a holocaust or sacrifice" and refers
to "the sacrifical ban" (1957:138,129). These scholars, however, are
in the minority in acknowledging the relationship between the ban
and sacrifice. The notion of the ban as sacrifice is not the only
banning model found in the Hebrew Scriptures (see chapter 2), but
the presence of the ban as sacrifice in the Hebrew Scriptures cannot
be denied.

Violent Death of One's Own versus
Killing the "Other": Martyrdom and the Ban

From whence does a conceptual thread such as the ban as sacrifice
come, culturally, psychoanalytically, historically, and what is its
significance for understanding ancient Israelites and their religion?
One special monograph in the study of Judaism should be mentioned in this context that explores with brilliance and sensitivity a

theme comparable to the ban in the literature and history of Judaism, that of human sacrifice and martyrdom. I refer to Shalom Spiegel's ground-breaking *The Last Trial*, a study of the story of the almost-sacrifice of Isaac in Genesis 22 and its subsequent understanding and development in the lore of post-biblical Rabbinic and medieval Judaism.

The near-sacrifice of Isaac like the suffering of the protagonist of Isaiah 53 comes to have atoning value in Judaism. When God plans to punish Israel for sinfulness, he will remember Abraham's willingness to offer his own son and the son's willingness to be offered and will stay his anger. Hence the interpretation of Ex 12:23 "And when He sees the blood" (i.e. the blood on the doorposts of Israelite and not Egyptian homes) in the Rabbinic commentary on Exodus, *Mekilta de Rabbi Ishmael* (Bo 7 and 12, ed. Friedmann 8a and 12a = Lauterbach I, pp. 57 and 88):

> He sees the blood of Isaac's Akedah, (Binding) as it is said (Gen 22:14) "And Abraham called the name of the place The Lord Seeth." Now elsewhere (1 Chron 21:15) it says, "And as he was about to destroy, the Lord beheld, and He repented Him of the evil." What did He behold? He beheld the blood of Isaac's Akedah, as it is said (Gen 22:8), "God will for Himself behold the lamb for a burnt offering" (Spiegel:52).

In an over-literalization of the verbal root "to see" that is properly translated at Gen 22:8, 14 as God "will provide," the midrash has Isaac become the lamb. Thus the destroyer, God, about to kill the first-born of the Egyptians is reminded of Abraham's ordeal and of Isaac's blood willingly offered and spares the first-born of the Israelites. Moreover, throughout history, the blood of Isaac will cause God's anger to turn from the deserved punishment of his people. In this way Isaac becomes the archetypal atoning martyr, but did he shed blood? Was Isaac not spared, after all, and is the tale of Genesis 22 in its current form not a rejection of child sacrifice and the offering of actual human blood? So Spiegel and most would say. What Spiegel shows, however, is that threads in the on-going tradition radically interpret Genesis 22 to mean that Isaac did shed blood. After all, note the Rabbis, when Abraham and Isaac ascend the mountain the verb is in the plural, but only Abraham is said to descend. Where was Isaac (Goldin:1–6)? Spiegel cites, for example, a tradition claiming that Isaac shed a quarter of his blood on the altar (44–48) and others that refer to Isaac's "ashes," as if he had been burnt as a sacrifice (43). Spiegel goes on to see connections between this thread in Rabbinic literary sources and later medieval sources from the period of the crusades, indicating that many Jews who took their own lives and those of their children rather than convert to Christianity believed themselves to be in imitation of the Akedah. Skillfully, Spiegel shows how ancient traditions of the sacrifice of Isaac serve as models of and models for self-sacrifice in the Mainz of 1096 (131–37). As Spiegel writes, "The boundaries between midrash and reality get blurred" (137). Spiegel not only traces this fascinating and troubling trajectory in Judaism, but asks the big question—where does the theme of the efficacy of human sacrifice come from? It is an important question also in the study of the ban, for if *ḥērem* was on some level regarded as human offering to the deity, the Akedah theme and the ban partake of the same essential world-view that regards the deity as appreciative of human sacrifices. Spiegel does not shy away from the implications of such a view of the deity. As Spiegel shows (78–79), the Rabbis themselves realized that such a thread was found in the Hebrew Scriptures.

Commenting on Mic 6:7, "Lo, I shall give my first born for my transgression," a Rabbinic tradition attributes these words to Mesha king of Moab who sacrifices his son in the heat of a difficult and losing battle against the Israelites. After the sacrifice the tables turn and the Moabites win (2 Kgs 3:21–27).

> He assembled all his astrologers and said to them: What is it about this nation that for them such miracles are performed? Why is it that I wage war with many nations and defeat them; but these Jews, they defeat me. Said the astrologers to him: It is all by merit of one elder they had, whose name was Abraham. When he was one hundred years old he was granted an only son; yet the father offered him up (to God). Said Mesha to them: *Did he actually carry that out?* They said to Mesha: *No.* Said he to them: If miracles were performed for his sake though he did not actually carry it out, imagine the consequences if he had carried it out? Well now, I too have a first-born son who is to succeed me on the throne. I am going to offer him up and maybe miracles will be

performed for our sake, as it is written, "Then he took his first-born son that should have reigned in his stead, and offered him for a burnt offering upon the wall" (2 Kgs 3:27).

As Spiegel notes (79–80),

> To be sure, the talmudic sages never wearied of repeating once and again what occurs again and once again in the Prophets: Which I commanded not, nor spoke it, neither came it into My mind" (Jer 19:5)—*I did not command* Jephthah to sacrifice his daughter, *I did not speak* to the king of Moab (saying) that he should sacrifice his son, *neither came it into My mind* to tell Abraham to slay his son. . . . Our Rabbis say: Why in connection with the king of Moab is the verb *speak* employed? Because the Holy One, blessed be He, said: Did I ever hold a conversation with him, etc.? Why, I never spoke so much as a word to him—and of all things, that he is to sacrifice his son? (*Tanhuma*, ed. Buber. *Wa-Yera* 50, p. 109; *Aggadat Bereshit*, Ch. 31, p. 63. See also b. *Taanit* 4a., *Gen. R* 55:5.)

So too, biblical texts such as Lev 18:21, 20:2–5; Deut 12:31, 18:10; Jer 7:30–31; 19:5 take a clear and unequivocal stance against human sacrifice as do poetic, possibly formulaic condemnations of those who slay children in the valleys, under the clefts of rocks (Isa 57:5; compare Ezek 20:25–26). The dominant voice in the Hebrew Bible condemns child sacrifice as the epitome of anti-Yahwist and anti-social behavior. In fact, the dominant voice in the Hebrew Bible treats the ban not as sacrifice in exchange for victory but as just and deserved punishment for idolators, sinners, and those who lead Israel astray or commit direct injustice against Israel. But as Morton Smith (1987) reminds us, the Hebrew Bible is dominated by particular ideologies that may well be at odds with the un-printed, cultural attitudes of the majority of Israelites who did not get the last word, and their attitudes are never completely covered up. They are found in polemics, in laden silences, in some of the methinks-he-doth-protest-too-much frameworks of the Hebrew Bible. Thus the Hebrew Bible insists that first-born humans not be offered in sacrifice but be redeemed (Ex 13:14, 15; see also Num 3:41, 45; Ex 34:19–20) side by side with the less nuanced statement that "Whatever is the first to open the womb among the Israelites, of human beings and animals, is mine" [Ex 13:2; see also Ex 22:29 (v. 28 in Hebrew)]. Narratives such as Genesis 22 also reveal a certain subversive attitude to human sacrifice.

Spiegel and most scholars read Genesis 22 as a condemnation of human offerings since, dramatically, Abraham's hand is stayed (see, for example, the treatment of O. Kaiser:48), but does the text condemn human sacrifice or do we want to read it that way? The neutrality of the narrator is, in fact, quite shocking. (See Maccoby:84, but compare 76.) No etiology is found such as "Hence we do not offer our children in sacrifice . . . ," no commentary directs this tale in a direction critical of child sacrifice. Rather, life is God's to give and take. He may on occasion demand the most valuable sacrifice a person can offer, a human who is his own child. Abraham's son is redeemed, a ram substituted, as the Israelites' firstborn are spared in the tale of Exodus, the blood on the doorposts being an adequate token substitute (or were the Egyptian children adequate to satiate the Destroyer's appetite?). Redemption and sacrifice are the two options, but the deity is imagined not always to redeem. Even when he redeems, something else is offered instead. The banned person is a sort of human sacrifice that cannot be redeemed, but if someone should dare to withhold God's ḥērem, he himself may become the unwilling substitute as in the prophet's interpretation of the Syrian king Ben-Hadad's escape from death (1 Kings 20).

As the tradition of human sacrifice is a recurring theme in Judaism, so the ban-as-sacrifice tradition is an on-going thread in ancient Israelite religion. The ideology of the ban is thus not an ancient or primitive view of warring that is later totally rejected, for Isaiah 34 testifies to its presence in a quite late poetic text, the symbol still intact. So Spiegel shows how the notion of divine forgiveness through the death of a child surfaces in eleventh-century reflections on the crusade.

Origins and Actualization

But what of the introduction of these conceptually related phenomena—the ban and child sacrifice—into Israelite religion, their earlier life, and what of actual praxis throughout Israel's history? The question of origins is a difficult one. Spiegel on child sacrifice and P. Stern on the ban are remarkably similar in writing of "pagan" origins. For Spiegel these ethically less evolved beliefs remain within the Israelite-Jewish tradition, retaining relevance for particular sociological and historical realities of persecution. Stern places the origin of *ḥērem* in a "polytheistic world," "a pagan world view which was adapted by Israel . . . and adjusted to Israel's peculiar religion" (Stern, 1989:93, 129; 1991:65). Both impute in this way a foreignness to the image of a God who accepts and desires child sacrifice or the ban.

To draw such a line between "alien" or "pagan" or "polytheistic" ideas and Israelite or Jewish ones is not as simple or accurately done a task as one might think. Many Israelites thought of themselves as Yahwists and yet veered from the normative monotheism that dominates the major written source, the Hebrew Scriptures. Now, one may wish to side with the Yahwists who had the final word and suggest that these looser folks were not really Israelites, religiously speaking, but that is to miss the richness and the full spectrum that was the ancient religion of Israel. The very polemics against these "subversive" beliefs testify to their presence among Israelites. Were such ideologies, grounded in the belief that God appreciates human sacrifice, enacted in the religious life of the Israelites? Were enemies promised to God by Israelites in actual wars? Were children actually sacrificed either on a regular basis— offering first-born children—or in irregular emergency circumstances when it was believed that the deity's attention and help required special invocation?

While there is still considerable controversy about the matter [see Morton Smith (1975) vs. Moshe Weinfeld (1978)], the consensus of scholars over the last decade concludes that child sacrifice was a part of ancient Israelite religion, to large segments of Israelite communities of various periods (Green:179, 187; Mosca; Heider; J. Day). Most modern scholars treat as separate phenomena hints concerning possible offerings of the first born (Ex 22:28; Ex 13:2, 14, 15) and suggestions that parents made their children "pass through the fire" as offerings to Molek (Heider:406; J. Day:85; Mosca:236-37) (Lev 18:21, 20:2-5; Jer 32:35; 2 Kings 23:10) though they make the point that both have to do with offering of human children in sacrifice to a deity; these phenomena are different manifestations of the same underlying belief in the efficacy of child sacrifice (Heider 265, 256–75; Mosca:235–36).

J. Day and Heider suggest that Molek was regarded by many Israelites as a god of the underworld and death. (For a differing treatment of the *mlk* root that nevertheless places it in a sacrificial context see Stager and Wolff:45.) Molek is mentioned in two Canaanite serpent charms (J. Day:84) and equated in Akkadian (Mesopotamian) sources with the god Nergal (J. Day:84). An ancient Near Eastern parallel for the cult of Molek is provided by Punic epigraphic and archaeological evidence (Heider:203). J. Day, Heider, and Mosca believe that the Molek cult took place in the valley of Hinnom at the Topheth (J. Day:83; Heider:405; Mosca: 220, 228), a word cognate with Aramaic and Syriac words meaning "fireplace," "oven," or "furnace" (J. Day:83).

Did Israelites offering children imagine themselves to be offering to a chthonic form of Yahweh? Many no doubt did as Heider allows (269, 272, 406) though J. Day denies it (85). Heider suggests that "the Molek sacrifices were surely irregular and voluntary. . . . It is possible that as was apparently true of the Punic offerings (of children to Molek), the sacrifices were performed in fulfillment of vows made to the deity (whether Yahweh, Molek, or the ancestors), and one may conjecture that, by the nature of the gift and the connections which scholars such as Pope have seen between the cults of love and death, the vows usually had to do with fertility" (406). Scholars who have explored the Molek-sacrifice in Israelite religion suggest that it is not merely a literary leftover from a pre-Israelite past or part of the belief system of a small renegade group of Israelites. Heider and Mosca conclude, in fact, that a form of child sacrifice was a part of state-sponsored ritual until the reform of the seventh-century BCE Judean king, Josiah, who eliminated the Topheth (Heider:406–7; Mosca:216, 238–39, 225).

The reign of the Judean king Josiah in the second half of the seventh century BCE is the time when many scholars believe that the large central portion of the Hebrew Bible from the Book of Deuteronomy through 2 Kings was collected and composed. The so-called Deuteronomic history includes older source materials of various dates, supplemented by Deuteronomic materials and shaped by the

Deuteronomists' compositional objectives. One of these objectives was a major religious reform that set the tone for what we now consider to be the mainstream biblical world-view. The Deuteronomic writers condemn the sacrifice of children. These are also the authors who have preserved and shaped much of the war-banning traditions of the Hebrew Scriptures. They must have been extremely uncomfortable with the ideology of vowing one's human enemies as an offering sacrificed to God. For these writers, the ban becomes something else that has to do with matters of justice and injustice, right and wrong, idolatry versus worship of the true God. One of the most central Deuteronomic themes is that of blessing versus curse: the good win God's blessing, the evil, God's curse (See Deut 27-28; 30:15-20). Ḥerem, the ban, becomes a form of enacting the punishment or curse for Israelites and non-Israelites alike. Idolaters are perceived as deserving of the ban.

And yet, the process of editing a work or compiling a collection in ancient times was not like modern censorship. The episode of the king of Moab's efficacious killing of his son is retained, for example, for the Rabbis to deal with later in the tradition. So the ban-as-sacrifice tradition remains visible, blended in with the ban as God's justice in some of the passages explored below. If, however, we are able to hypothesize about those who present the ban as justly imposed punishment for sinners—we will discuss their motivations and the implications of their world-view in more detail in chapter 2—what can we say about those who saw the ban as sacrifice? Again we return to basic questions. Does this ideology reflect a way real wars were fought at some point in Israel's history? Who, then, was in control of the violence? Or can we speak only of ideology—a way of wanting to understand the conquest of land? If so, who would want to understand Israel's early history this way? Perhaps the answer to a less Israelite-bound question might lead to understanding a puzzle specific to Israelite culture.

How and for Whom Is the Ban as Sacrifice Meaningful?

What psychological needs are served by the ban as sacrifice? The ban validates the enemy as human and valuable and does not turn him into a monster worthy of destruction, a cancer that must be rooted out. The enemy is not the unclean "other," but a mirror of the self, that which God desires for himself. Comparisons with the human sacrifice-martyrdom theme are again useful. Imposition of the ban, so that dead enemies become an offering to God, is one way of making sense of the inevitable carnage of war as considering the martyr's death to be a means of awakening divine attention and assuring forgiveness is a way of making sense of a mob's murder of family and friends. (Compare Maccoby:81). The deaths cannot be for nothing, meaningless. The ban as sacrifice deals with the guilt of the killers rather than the grief of the bereaved. The guilt involved in killing human beings is well documented in studies of actual wars (Hendin and Hass:33–36, 65–66, 149, 157–59, 160–82). People and their cultures deal with the horror of having taken human life in various ways. The enemy may be perceived as a "Gook," an Infidel, an "Other," not of human stock. The ban as sacrifice accepts that the slaughter of the enemy in a successful battle is the killing of actual humans like oneself, but treats the deaths as necessary offerings to God, required if the battle is to succeed. But why kill everyone? The ban as sacrifice has a terrifying completeness and fairness about it. Because all has been promised to God, there is no individual decision that need be made about sparing this person or that, no guilt about tactical or surgical strikes that go awry. All people are condemned and the matter is out of one's hands.

Paradoxically, the ban as sacrifice may be viewed as admitting of more respect for the value of human life than other war ideologies that allow for the arbitrary killing of soldiers and civilians. This suggestion puts one in the uncomfortable position of appearing somehow sympathetic to the ban as sacrifice. Any of us, of course, would prefer to face an enemy who held to an ideology of war allowing for mercy, restraint, or haphazard escape, but one is trying to understand and enter into the world-view of those who could espouse such a rigid ideology of war. The ban as sacrifice requires a wider view of a God who appreciates human sacrifice, so those who would partake in the ideology of the ban would presumably have something in common with those who believed in the efficacy of child sacrifice. Such a world-view continues throughout Israel's history as indicated by polemics against child sacrifice and by late texts such as Isaiah 34 that associate God with the sacrifice of dead warriors.

Self-conceptions Implied by Images
of the Ban as Sacrifice

In the trajectory of texts isolated above the ban is invoked to gain God's help in conquering territory, a political objective more typical of societies with governments than of societies without governments. On the other hand, the ban might appeal ecologically to less sophisticated groups unable to absorb large numbers of new people as opposed to, for example, slave-holding empires. The banning texts cited all have to do with non-Israelite enemies. As noted above, such complete ways of annihilating an enemy in various cultures are reserved for those considered outside of the group. The dichotomy between Israel and non-Israel is very clear in the ban as sacrifice. Such clarity in defining the group as well as the interest in territorial objectives might date the attitudes implicit in these texts to a point in Israel's history at which some group thinks of itself as whole, a threatened whole, but a whole nevertheless. The use of the term "Israel" for the group may well be anachronistic, but the ban-as-sacrifice ideology contrasts "inside the group" with "outside the group," and war, largely understood to be the taking of others' territory, involves distinguishing what belongs to "our" group from what belongs to "theirs." The ban is not shown to be employed by Israelite kings making vows to God—hence de Vaux (1961b) and others' suggestions that it is an old religious ideology replaced by the profane pragmatism of the state. But how old is old?

Israelite Origins and the Ban as Sacrifice

This line of reasoning about those to whom the ban as sacrifice might have been a meaningful ideology of war raises hotly debated issues concerning the origins and early social history of the people Israel. Until the seventies, two suggestions were generally offered by scholars. One hypothesis posits a conquest of the land of Canaan by outsiders who would become Israel. Archaeological evidence is cited as proof that the general picture of burning, strafing, and take-over portrayed by the biblical book of Joshua is accurate, even if Joshua's depiction of specific battles for specific towns such as Jericho is not accurate. This hypothesis, made famous by William Foxwill Albright, is still offered in some form by works such as Bright's *History* (3rd ed.:133–43). The conquest model, however, is not accepted by the majority of contemporary scholars who suggest it relies on a forced equation between archaeological evidence and the Bible's ideologically grounded narrative agenda. Another older theory of origins also now generally rejected is the "infiltration model." This theory (like some versions of the conquest) accepts that the Israelites were originally nomads from the desert who infiltrated the highlands of Israel. These various groups of settlers entered slowly over time, and gradually unified into an Israelite league, sharing belief in Yahweh, the God of the covenant. Scholars no longer accept that Israel originally consisted of nomads who left the steppe to settle down in the land and have become much more sophisticated about forms of nomadism and the cross-overs that occur between nomadic and sedentary life-styles; nor is Martin Noth's theory of an Israelite amphictyony or league accepted uncritically (de Geus).

Current work is influenced by methodological concerns and approaches discussed in the introduction: the defining of terms such as tribe, nomad, and lineage (de Geus; Lemche; Gottwald, 1979); the characteristics of pre-state and state societies (Coote and Whitelam; de Geus); the importance of issues of economic status, class, urban versus rural (Mendenhall; Gottwald, 1979) in understanding Israelite origins; the concern with factors of ecology—scarcity, population growth, food supply, climate, and economics (Coote and Whitelam; Frick, 1985).

Two models have developed out of these sorts of anthropological and economic approaches, the revolt model and the pioneer-settlement model. The former suggests that Israel emerged from within the land as poor highland peasants who revolt against urban Canaanite overlords holding power at least nominally as vassals of Egypt. The catalyst for and "the brains" of this revolt is a small group of former slaves, mercenaries, and bandits who escape from Egypt. Their unifying ideology is covenantal Yahwism. The "have-not" indigenous population of Canaan is attracted to this ideology.

Together the newcomers and the local population overthrow the "haves."

The pioneer-settlement model as outlined by Coote and Whitelam suggests that the highlands population in the late Bronze and early Iron Ages (ca. late fourteenth, early thirteenth century BCE) consisted of "a crucial-mix of nomads, bandits, and village communities . . . outside the reach of state power but dependent on Jerusalemite commerce." (129) These groups do not come from elsewhere but have long been established in Canaan. They compete with one another and either compete with the forces of urban power in the highlands (cf. Gottwald, 1979) or serve the ruling classes as strongmen selling protection, merchant traders, and so on. With the reduction of eastern Mediterranean trade in the late Bronze Age, the "crucial-mix" highland groups lose their source of income. To survive, highland bandit and tribal leaders stop fighting among themselves and join the peasants moving into an alternate means of support, subsistence agriculture. "The political form that achieved and maintained" the "stay of conflict" between these highland groups was referred to eventually by its adherents with the name Israel (Coote and Whitelam, 1987:131). The settlement model allows that certain leaders or chieftains would emerge. The various villages, bandit and nomadic groups, no doubt, would have had such leaders even before the formation of these more state-like societies. The pioneer-settlement theory is least tied to the biblical sources of the four theories of Israel's origins depending instead on archaeological evidence and ethnographic and economic models from non-Israelite cultures.

The identification of the ban as sacrifice ideology does not help to confirm one or another of these theories. In the conquest theory, the ideology of the ban would support an insurgent group's attempts to eliminate alien populations. The insurgent group would regard the killing and the destruction as a sacrifice demanded by God (see Eibl-Eibesfeldt:185, chapter 1 and discussion in chapter 6). In the infiltration model, the ban might be imposed in defensive wars, to protect newly settled holdings. The "group" that shares the ideology and protects itself need not be a whole Israel, but one or more of the smaller groups that later unified to become Israel. The same applies to Coote and Whitelam's smaller groups and early confederations in the settlement model.

The ideologically charged, strongly Yahwistic group united under the covenant and seeking liberation from oppressors would seem less likely to adhere to a ban-as-sacrifice ideology than an ideology of ban as God's justice, to be discussed below. Scholars sympathetic to the settlement model suggest that Gottwald and Mendenhall have over-idealized Israel's origins in accordance with themes of oppression and liberation now present in biblical narrative. Perhaps they are right.

Ideology, Actuality, and Chronology

In any event, it seems safe at least to conclude that before kingship in Israel, smaller bands who were part of what Israel would become clearly identified themselves as groups—whether any called themselves by the name "Israel" or not. Warrior chiefs or judges might well have had the same status and authority as a petty tyrant such as Mesha of Moab to lead their group to war, and to invoke the ban in efforts to preserve or expand their fragile hegemony. And yet, the move from ideology preserved in sacred writings to historical actualities is, in fact, a great leap. We can never be certain if Israelite rulers of any period ever invoked the ban against actual enemies. The ban-as-sacrifice ideology seems as if it would find an appropriate matrix in earliest Israelite or pre-Israelite culture. It is, of course, entirely possible that some Israelite and Judean kings with their followers continued to partake of the ban-as-sacrifice ideology and that they actually imposed the ban on enemies. Mesha the Moabite, after all, dates to the ninth century BCE, well into the period of the Israelite and Judean monarchies. If Israelite and Judean kings did enact this ideology in actual wars, however, they are not so portrayed by biblical writers. Are biblical writers unaware of such monarchic banning traditions? Have they covered them up, while projecting the ban as sacrifice back, before the monarchy, into what they regard as or portray as earlier, more primitive times? Might the ban be not a "triumphant ideology" (Hanson:44) to such writers, but a bit of an embarrassment, safely consigned to olden times? This line of reasoning is, of course, extremely hypothetical and points to the difficulties of matching ancient literature with ancient history. The literary evidence of the

Hebrew Bible suggests that an Israelite ideology of the ban as sacrifice could be as old as Israel and that it is retained in some form through the late biblical period when Isaiah 34 was composed. About the actual conduct of wars we cannot know. The ideology of the ban as sacrifice is joined and, in fact, overshadowed in the Hebrew Scriptures by a different conception of the ban, that of the ban as God's justice.

2

The Ban As God's Justice

The ideology of the ban as sacrifice never disappears in Israelite thought as noted above, but side by side with it in the Hebrew Scriptures, indeed overpowering it, is the related and transformed ideology of the ban as God's justice. The Deuteronomic writers, supporters of the Josianic reform, consider the ban a means of rooting out what they believe to be impure, sinful forces damaging to the solid and pure relationship between Israel and God.

As the story of the reform goes (2 Kings 22), during the reign of a young and good king Josiah, a "book of the law" is found in the temple which is undergoing repairs. The book explains to Josiah the reason for all of Israel's recent failings: "Great is the wrath of the Lord that is kindled against us because our ancestors did not obey the words of this book." (2 Kgs 22:8) The king undertakes a reform. The finding of a "book of truth" [the meaning of this event is further explained by the prophetess Hulda (2 Kgs 22:14-20)] is a common cross-cultural motif, but we assume Josiah's reform to have been an actual event in Israel's history, governed by a particular set of beliefs and values. Josiah and his supporters whom many scholars regard as the intellectual offspring of similarly minded, conservative Northern Israelite reformers of the previous two centuries (G.E. Wright, 1953:320–26; for a thorough review of the history of scholarship concerning the Deuteronomistic tradition see O'Brien:3–23 and McKenzie, 1991:1–19, 122–34) seek to rid Israelite religion of what they regard to be idolatrous, contaminating, and degenerate practices. Such fanatic and witch-hunting reforms in response to difficult economic, political, or cultural realities are not unique to Israelite history. In any event, Josiah's reforming activities are outlined in 2 Kings 23. Among them is the defiling of the Topheth where people are said to have made their sons and daughters "cross over" or "pass through" the fire to Molek, who was either an independent deity or regarded as a chthonic aspect Yahweh himself (see chapter 1). Other practices regarded as idolatrous by these writers are listed and associated with various foreigners—e.g. "Astarte the detestable one of the Sidonians, Chemosh the detestable one of Moab, and Milcom, the abomination of the Ammonites" (23:13).

On the one hand, as modern readers we sympathize with and are proud of the Deuteronomists for their rejection of child sacrifice, for not imagining their God as desirous of human offerings. On the other hand we should be conscious that our own world-view is, in part, shaped by these ancient biblical writers. They may have been ready to dub "idolatrous" practices or life-styles that other biblical authors or we—had we lived then—might have been content to consider within the purview of the "real" Yahwism. These are the writers for whom the ban becomes not a means of gaining God's favor through offering human booty, but a means of gaining God's favor through expurgation of the abomination, through justly deserved punishment of the subversive enemy, external to the people Israel or internal.

The Deuteronomic writers place the ban in a just war context. Using the phrase "just war" invokes Johnson's point about the blurring of Bainton's categories of just war and crusade, when the war is regarded as commanded by God, a means of establishing his justice. The war is not limited—no *jus in bello* pertains—but the war is justified, claimed to be fought for a just and Godly cause. In the process of making this argument for war, the Deuteronomic writers show themselves sensitive to and concerned with the ban-as-sacrifice tradition. It does not suit their world-view. They, like Peter Craigie, Robert Good, Norman Gottwald and others implicitly ask how God can be envisioned to demand such blood-letting. Their answer has become the answer accepted by most modern scholars who try to understand the place of the ban in Israelite religion: divine judgment. We have uncovered an alternate trajectory, the ban as sacrifice, but turn now to the ban texts that emphasize issues of God's justice and the enemies' deserved punishment. In a few of these passages, the ban-as-sacrifice ideology remains and predominates, but is joined by indications that the ban is also perceived as an imposition of divine justice. The two trajectories are found in the Achan incident (Joshua 7) and in the confrontation between Samuel and Saul at I Sam 15:1–33. The brief references to issues of justice in these passages may be Deuteronomic additions to inherited traditions, but one cannot be certain. These texts are, in any event, witness to the fact that for some biblical writers, the ban as sacrifice as found in 1 Kings 20 or Num 21:2–3 is not a conceptually adequate or satisfying explanation for this form of total annihilation.

Jericho and Achan

The battle of Jericho (Joshua 6) is interesting from many perspectives. First, the battle scene is rich in nuances of ritual preparation and engagement: the seven priests carrying seven ram's horns before the ark; the blowing of trumpets; the marching in magic circles around the city on six days, with a seven-time circling on the holy and whole seventh day; the fact that Joshua meets the commander of the Lord's army before the battle to be held on "holy ground" (Josh 5:13–15). So Ashurbanipal is charged to battle by Ishtar, her sword drawn, in an Assyrian version of this formulaic pre-battle vision experience. Joshua, like Moses (Ex 3:5), is told to take off his shoes, for the place where he stands is holy. This scene thus finds its place in Israelite and wider ancient Near Eastern theophanic and war traditions. The victory, moreover, is a miracle account and though Israelites fight and kill with swords, the notion that the battle is God's and the victory won by God is very strong. In some of the biblical texts to be presented in chapter 7 the idea of God's fighting becomes linked to a primitive kind of pacifism in which human beings do not and need not raise their hands in war.

Embedded in the tale of the battle for Jericho is the story of Rahab, the harlot with the heart of gold who saves the Israelite spies, reversing the unfortunate events of Numbers 13, and who as a non-Israelite declares and confirms God's power. The Pharaoh of

Genesis 41, Balaam of Numbers, the Gibeonites of Joshua 9, and Naaman in 2 Kings 5 play similar roles. The foreigner's approval is often presented as the surest proof of divine omnipotence which is interesting in and of itself. Only Rahab and her family escape the fate of the ban. The theme of paying one's due is at the heart of the ban as sacrifice and is found also in the Rahab episode. Her kindness and conversion are rewarded with life (Josh 6:17). All the remaining living beings of Jericho, men and women, young and old, oxen and donkeys, are doomed to die under the ban, devoted to God for destruction presumably in return for his defeat of the city. All silver, gold, and bronze vessels (v.19) go to the Lord's treasury, a sacred offering. This act of devotion under the ban is among the most complete in biblical war portrayals. Should anyone break the ban and take devoted things for himself, Israel's own camp will be substituted and become banned (Josh 6:18). The vow must not be broken; any loss to God must be covered by a substitute donation. Achan, however, cannot resist the valuables and takes some of the spoil for himself. As a result, God does not support Israel in the battle with Ai and they suffer defeat.

God speaks to Joshua. Israel has transgressed the covenant "my bĕrît" (Josh 7:11). The terms of the deal have been broken. Israel has "stolen" God's things, God's ḥērem, the loot devoted to him. God will not continue to fight alongside Israel unless they transfer God's ḥērem to him, the mode of transfer being destruction (Josh 7:12, 13). Achan, who has taken the forbidden things and, indeed, his entire household, have now become part of the ḥērem as predicted in the warning of Josh 6:18. The shocking list of that which is to be annihilated includes Achan, what he has stolen, his sons and daughters, oxen, donkeys, sheep, and all he had (Josh 7:24). The text veers from singular to plural in vv. 25–26 in referring to those who are killed, a scribal oscillation perhaps stemming from discomfort with the totality of the destruction, but it is clear that at least one tradition, the one that links up best with v. 24, imagines Achan and all that belongs to him burned with fire and stoned by stones in the protective enclosure of the Valley. Achan has been made an example of what happens to people who steal God's ḥērem, who break the treaty promise to give all. Like the merchant of "Beauty and the Beast" who steals the beast's rose, the merchant or his substitute becomes forfeit. Once the balance is restored and

God has his *ḥērem* and additional compensation besides, Israel can be victorious against Ai.

The Achan incident partakes of a recurring biblical pattern of transgression and punishment and is in this way a very important marker of the way in which the two *ḥērem* trajectories converge. That which is banned is a sacrifice, devoted to God who must have his due, but the ban is also understood as a means of rooting out the cancerous and contagious "other," that which is unclean because of sin. Achan must die because he has transgressed covenant and done *nĕbālāh*, an outrageous thing (7:15).

René Girard would find in the Achan episode an excellent example of the mythic pattern of the scapegoat.

> A community that actively seeks and finds scapegoats is usually a community troubled by dissension or by some real or imaginary disaster. Such a community will establish a false causal link between its chosen scapegoat and the real or imaginary cause of its trouble, whatever that may be. The presence in all these myths of some disaster for which the victim is regarded as at least objectively, if not also personally, responsible could certainly result from the community's state of panic and from the systematic projections of all scapegoaters onto their scapegoats (Girard, 1987:103).

Thus the people at first lose the battle with Ai, panic and lose heart, but find a cause for their failure, unifying in the effort to identify and eliminate him, and finally in the aftermath of his death, succeed in their battle. Aspects of scapegoating as described so perceptively by Girard are certainly found in the ideology of ban as God's justice as a whole (see below and Girard 1987:74, 86-87, 98, 132). The notion of *ḥērem* as God's property, his sacrifice, however, dominates this passage. The term "covenant" seems to refer not to the larger relationship with God but specifically to the deal, the war-vow, especially in v. 11. The burning of Achan and his household is evocative of a sacrificial scene. He has become *ḥērem*, a part of that which is devoted, but a thread of this passage also understands *ḥērem* as judgment, a justified war to root out sin. In fact, the two concepts are contradictory as J. Pedersen muses in some confusion (Vol 4:331-32; see also Stern, 1989:156; 1991:104). How can that which is unclean be a sacral offering to God? Girard would suggest,

I think, that the scapegoat is, in fact, both hated and respected by those who kill him (again enter themes of mimesis), presenting examples of scapegoats such as Oedipus who come to acquire sacred status (1987:94, 96, 114–115). Perhaps it is in the myth of scapegoating that ideologies of the ban as sacrifice and the ban as God's justice sometimes find a border or meeting ground. There is in any event a real tension in the tradition. Most of the passages that emphasize the uncleanness issue do not participate in the ban-as-sacrifice trajectory. The tension between the two traditions found in the Jericho/Achan narrative is found, however, also in the scene concerning Agag in 1 Sam 15:1–33.

Saul and Agag

This scene, in fact, evidences two sorts of tension: the tension between the ideology of statecraft and the ban—or perhaps between more or less rigorous interpretations of the ban—and the tension between the ban as sacrifice and the ban as a rooting out of that which is unclean and sinful. At 1 Sam 15:3 Samuel delivers God's word to Saul to put Amalek under the ban. The formulaic chain of those to be destroyed, the multiple verbs of destruction, and the contrast between the ban and "sparing" (another of these terms connoting "ransom," "redeem," "save") are all found. Also found, however, is just cause for the massive execution. The Lord "pays attention to" [a special verb meaning "pay attention to bad deeds in order to punish them" (*pqd*)] "what Amalek did to Israel, setting against/blocking their path as they went up from Egypt" (1 Sam 15:2). Amalek has maltreated Israel and is being punished via the ban.

Saul does kill all the people "by the edge of the sword" in the usual enactment of the ban. But Agag the king and the best of the animals and "all that was of worth" they spared and "were not willing to devote to destruction" (1 Sam 15:9). That which was regarded as worthless, however, they did devote. This is, of course, to misunderstand the ban and to devalue human life itself. God's offering is that which is most valuable. To mix humans, the highest of God's breathing creations, with sickly or less valuable animals is to break the whole concept of the ban as sacrifice. Similarly, to offer all humans but spare the king, the prize as head of his people, and to offer the animals of lesser worth and spare the best is the opposite of what is required under the ban.

Samuel confronts Saul who claims in his defense that he intends to offer the animals as regular sacrifices to God later, but this is not adequate. From *zĕbāḥîm*, sacrifices of the sort Saul mentions (1 Sam 15:15) one makes a feast and enjoys eating meat from the sanctified flesh. That devoted to destruction is not to be shared with God in any sense. Samuel tells Saul that he has swooped down upon—literally "wrapped himself up in" (1 Sam 15:19)—the spoil. Again this passage emphasizes that Agag and his people are deserving of death. They are called sinners (cf. Jer 50:14; 1 Sam 15:18). The need to establish justice and recompense evil is especially strong in Samuel's final condemnation of Agag at 15:33. "As your sword has bereaved women so your mother will be the most bereaved of women." The issue is one of equity and fairness; the issue is not the deal with God, a vow of humans paid for victory. At work is an implicit expectation that war will be fought for a just cause. This passage departs significantly from ban-as-sacrifice texts and appeals to a quite different ethic. The ban has become a punishment for unethical behavior, a matter of vengeance. And yet, even so, the sacrifice nuance is found in this text in the imperfect ban of vv. 8–9, defended by Saul at v. 15 but rejected by the prophet, and finally in Samuel's killing of Agag. 1 Sam 15:33 states that Saul hewed up Agag before the Lord in Gilgal. The verb for "hewing" is used only here, but the image of cutting in pieces is strongly reminiscent of the ritual preparation of sacrificial animals—an image strengthened by the phrase "before the Lord at Gilgal," a cult center. (On the association of the latter phrase with cultic activity see Fowler:384–90; also Green:164).

Covenantal Framework for the Ban as God's Justice

One of the biblical war passages most attentive to issues of justice is Deut 13:12–18 (vv. 13–19 in the Hebrew). Justice is understood in Deuteronomic, strongly covenantal terms. To worship other gods and be faithless to Yahweh is to tear asunder the moral fabric of the Israelite world. It is to commit abomination (13:13) [v. 14 in the

Hebrew] as an ingrate to the God who has rescued and sustained his people. Deuteronomy 13 contains the most literal reference to the ban as sacrifice, calling the utter destruction, *kālîl,* "a whole burnt offering to the Lord, your God" (13:16) [v. 17 in the Hebrew]. The overriding issue in this passage, however, is justice under the covenant and with the one exception of the Achan episode, in contrast to the texts explored thus far, the ban is to be imposed on brother and sister Israelites.

If the Israelites hear that in one of their cities reprobates or base fellows have negatively influenced, literally "impelled," the inhabitants of their city saying "let us go and worship other gods that you have not known" then the ban is not immediately invoked, but with a genuine juridical procedure the matter is to be "searched out" and "investigated" and "questioned well" and if the accusation turns out to be true then the ban is to be imposed. The passage gives no indication of the political machinery that directs the investigation or declares the ban necessary. Much in Deuteronomy is of a theoretical nature, like the second-century Jewish law code, the Mishnah, often planning for a reality that no longer or does not yet exist.

The formulaic banning language of striking with the edge of the sword appears at v. 15 (v. 16 in the Hebrew) as does the *ḥrm* "ban" term itself. In this case, as in the somewhat comparable Achan episode, all booty of the town is to be gathered in the center of the town square and the town is to be burned to annihilation (13:16) [v. 17 in the Hebrew] never to be rebuilt. Nothing of that which is banned is to "stick to your hands in order that God turn from his anger and bestow you mercy, and be merciful to you and make you numerous as he swore to your ancestors" (13:17) [v. 18 in the Hebrew]. Thus the blessings of plenty and mercy follow the restoration of covenant, threatened by the polytheistic behavior of one town, the "bad seed" in the group. The case is carefully investigated in the Achan incident as well, through the divinatory means of casting lots, and burning is the means of final annihilation. Staying away from that which is banned is mentioned in Deuteronomy 13, the keeping of banned booty in the context of war having been the cause of the banning of Achan and his family in Joshua 7. And so there are similarities between these inner-Israelite episodes.

The Achan episode with its double references to covenant-breaking (Josh 7:11, 15) moves in the direction of understanding the ban

as a means of imposing justice, but Joshua 7 places greater emphasis on giving God his due, insisting above all that Achan has stolen
that which was devoted to God. Deuteronomy 13, even given its
overt reference to the ban as a whole burnt offering, clearly places
the ban in the context of a war to assert God's judgment, a defense
of the faith, in short a crusade.

It is important to take note of the totality of the ban in Deuteronomy 13 as in the elimination of Achan and his household. All booty
is utterly destroyed. It is no coincidence that the bans against fellow
Israelites are the only cases in which any enjoyment of spoil is
forbidden to human beings. In the case of Jericho, valuable inanimate booty is denied to Israelites, but goes to "the Lord's treasury"
which at least has human executors. In Joshua 7 and Deuteronomy
13, no priest and no Israelite is to benefit from the spoil. Several
issues are involved here. (1) The matter of imposing the ban on kin.
To suggest conducting wars of extermination against members of
one's own group betokens an out-of-kilter, poorly functioning society or a society in transition. (2) The matter of guilt and killing, in
particular when killing fellow Israelites. (3) Concepts of purity. The
ideology of the ban as God's justice responds in different ways than
the ideology of the ban as sacrifice to these issues. Most striking
about the texts in the trajectory of the ban as God's justice is the
emphasis they place on reasons for the killing. The many banning
texts discussed in chapter 1 offer no right-is-on-our-side explanation of the ban. Idolatry and the worship of other gods are clearly
offered as reasons for the imposition of the ban in the lawsuit-like
Deuteronomy 13. If worship of other gods is alleged, the accusation
is thoroughly investigated and if found to be true, a sentence is
issued and carried out. The sentence is the ban.

Similarly, the Hebrew text of Ex 22:19 (v. 20 in Greek) presents
the ban as just punishment for idolatry: "He who sacrifices to the
gods will be 'devoted to destruction' unless it be to Yahweh alone."
As the awkwardness of the language suggests, this verse is problem-
atical. The Hebrew words for "other" and "ban" are very similar,
and some confusion may have arisen in the transmission of the text.
One ancient Greek manuscript tradition for this verse can be understood to omit the "banning" language, reading "Whoever sacrifices
to other gods will surely die" (Alt:311, n. 2). The Hebrew Masoretic
tradition thus may reflect a scribal aberration that nevertheless

made sense to a writer prepared to understand the ban in Deuteronomic terms.

In Deut 7:2-5, the demand that the people of the land be banned (7:2) and not be pitied ("to pity" being the opposite of the ban) is accompanied by orders that no connections are to be made with the foreigners and no treaties, for treaties lead to intermarriage, and intermarriage to the worship of the foreign spouse's god—to contamination of the specially chosen, sacred people (see 7:3-4, 6). The themes of purity and separation and the cause of God's justice are very clear.

In Deut 7:23-26, the *ḥērem* as referring to banned objects becomes synonymous with "the abomination," the silver or gold that had covered the enemies' idols. It is not clear in the transition from 7:24 to 7:25 that the phrase the "images of their gods" refers specifically to war spoil and therefore material doomed under the ban in war. Rather, anything associated with the worship of other gods is rendered *ḥērem* in and of itself—a source of uncleanness that must be safely set apart and destroyed, for it is veritably contagious: "Do not bring an abomination into your house and become *ḥērem* (banned) like it" (Deut 7:26). The language of revulsion is visceral: You must detest it and abhor it for it is *ḥērem*.

Some of the texts in which the ban involves just cause refer not to idolatry, but to the unfairness of the enemy. The description of the dispossessing of Sihon of Heshbon in Deut 2:26-35 is couched in terms of the sort of war action in a just cause that is more carefully outlined in Deuteronomy 20, which looks like a rudimentary war code. Moses offers terms of peace. He requests merely the right of travel through Sihon's land, promising to keep to the highway and to pay for any food and water necessary for his people (2:27-28). But Sihon refuses this request, presented by the author in the most reasonable and gentlemanly terms, and renders himself worthy of the ban (2:33-35).

More accurately, like the Pharaoh of the Exodus, he has been made to refuse by God in order that he become deserving of destruction (Deut 2:30). The same juxtaposition of the ban with the hardening of the enemy ruler's heart is found in the summary line at Josh 11:20. The war ideology in both cases assumes that the ban is invoked for just cause—the enemy deserves it because of its own aggression or injustice. And yet this very rational-seeming attitude combines with an equally strong assumption that God controls the disposition of war and whether or not the ban will be imposed; decisions on the part of the king of Heshbon and the rest are not their own, for the land is destined to become the holding of Israel; even so that land is taken with attention to some rules of just cause and pre-war conduct.

It is interesting to compare the version of the encounter with Sihon found in Deuteronomy 2 with that of Num 21:21–25. The Numbers version also makes the case for the reasonableness of Moses' appeal to Sihon. Moses promises more briefly that his people will not disturb vineyards or native wells, but Sihon refuses and is put to the sword, his land taken by Israel. No ban is invoked or implemented, however. In the Numbers version, the ban is not a form of punishment, a way in which judgment is imposed upon the inhospitable resister of Israel's divine destiny.

Neatening Up War Ideologies: Deuteronomy 20

The Deuteronomic interest in finding just causes for the imposition of the ban finds fullest expression in the code of Deuteronomy 20. This war text reiterates and extends the reasoning of Deut 7:2–5: contact with the peoples of the land leads to abomination and sin, for they will "teach you to do all the abhorrent things they do for their gods" (20:18). Deut 20:10–18, however, also reveals an attempt to make sense of the disparate war traditions, reflected in biblical accounts of a conquest of the land. Why, for example, is the ban imposed on Arad at Num 21:2–3 and not on Sihon at Num 21:24? Why is livestock taken as spoil in some cases but not in others?

Deut 20:10–18 assumes the form of a code for wars of conquest as part of a larger code that describes the make-up of the Israelite armed force, the role of the priest and others officials in preparing troops formally for the battle (20:1–9), the treatment of trees in conquered territories (20:19–20) and of captured women (21:10–14), and the disposition of the army camp in regard to matters of purity (23:9–14). Deut 20:10–18 is actually an effort to neaten up traditions preserved in the literature of the Hebrew Bible, reflecting varying war ideologies. [See the treatment of Fishbane (200) who regards the more lenient tradition as the earlier and Rofé's redaction-critical study (1985:26–29).] One tradition allows towns targeted for conquest to submit and accept peace terms that nevertheless enslave its citizens. If the town will not submit, its males are to be put to the sword, while its women, children, livestock, and everything else in the town may be taken as booty. The latter is, in general, the way of war described for the monarchic period in the Hebrew Scriptures. While the wars for most of the monarchic period are generally not imperialistic and initiated to conquer territory, nevertheless, once there is war and enemy territory falls, males are killed, women and children taken. Deut 20:16–18 describes, in contrast, the imposition of the ban in which no living things are to survive. The basis of the distinction between the ways in which enemies are to be treated is geographic. Those peoples from "very far away" areas are to be given the chance to live (20:15), but those within "Israel's inheritance" must die lest they influence Israel to turn away from God.

The geographic distinction is very much in tune with other aspects of the war code in Deuteronomy, and betokens a particular world-view. The army is to be a whole in mind and body safely fenced off from those whose attention might be elsewhere (20:5–8) and from acts of impropriety (23:9) (Pedersen:1–10). The camp is to be clean and holy, a sacred space, another whole (Pedersen:12; Douglas:1–57). Rules for conquest too assume a neatly defined division between the area within the destined whole, the land of Israel, and the area outside. The contours of this particular whole, of course, are subject to change depending upon the biblical tradition followed. In any event, the Deuteronomic prescriptions do not adequately account for inconsistencies in the way the ban is imposed in the Hebrew Bible (Gottwald, 1964:299), especially in a book such as Numbers which is outside the Deuteronomic corpus. Deut 20:15–18 does tell us a great deal about the Deuteronomic ideology of the ban—a view, as Gottwald has noted, that suits a "cultic conception" of Israel "as a single people sharply separated in religious practice from all the nations" (1964: 303, 305; see also Stulman:614)). The ideology of the ban as God's justice suits particular periods in Israel's history, particular threads in Israelite culture, particular sorts of groups. We have identified the seventh-century BCE Deuteronomic reformers as the core who preserved and shaped this version of the ban, allowing both for their ideological precursors and their offspring in the tradition.

The emphasis on the enemy's deserving to be banned, on divine judgment, and on the need to preserve the wholeness of the people Israel is found, for example, also in Jeremiah's response to the cataclysmic events of the Babylonian conquest of the Judean kingdom in 586 BCE. Jeremiah's career would have, in fact, begun during the reign of Josiah and the hypothesized Deuteronomic reform. The Deuteronomists attempt to provide a covenantally based theoretical framework for the ban traditions of the conquest thereby covertly reflecting and affecting contemporary attitudes of the seventh and sixth centuries BCE. Jeremiah overtly writes of the ban to be imposed against the sixth-century oppressor Babylon. Babylon "the plunderer" (Jer 50:11) who has "sinned against the Lord" (Jer 50:14) is to be punished (50:18); God's vengeance is upon her (50:15). She is to be placed under the ban (50:26). Sacrificial nuances enter at 50:10 that juxtapose the language of satiation (*śbʿ*) and plunder and at 50:27 in which the imposition of the ban is equated with images of bulls going to the slaughter. The dominant ban trajectory in Jeremiah as in the Deuteronomic passages discussed above is, however, that of God's justice.

The ban as God's justice is a controversial and dangerous ideology, clothed in the respectable concept of covenant. In the Deuteronomists' theoretical system, the ban appears to be controlled by juridical cautions and concerns, a guardian of a united, whole, and pure Israel, a means of combating the enemies of purity, internal and external. Joshua 22 shows the controlled ban ideology at work. While Joshua 22 does not use the term *ḥrm*, except in a telling reference to Achan's sin of stealing from banned booty, "God's *ḥērem*" (22:20), the passage purports to give an example of the sort of inner Israelite case calling for the ban as described in Deut 13:12–17. The Reubenites, Gadites, and half-tribe of Manasseh are accused of engaging in subversive worship involving an altar in their territory across the Jordan (on textual and source problems, especially in the tribes' interesting self-defense at 22:22–23 see Boling, 1982:508, 515 and Niditch, 1982:374–75). The procedure outlined in Deuteronomy 13 is shown to work well in Joshua 22. The case is investigated, the charges prove to be false, and the tribes return to their side of the Jordan in peace.

The Ban Gone Awry: Critique?

The tale in Judges 19–21, however, provides a perspective on the advice of Deuteronomy 13 gone awry. In the repetitive, economical prose of traditional-style literature a narrator spins a tale. A woman has left her husband, a Levite residing in Ephraim, and returns to her father's house in Bethlehem. The husband goes after her and wins her back, remaining with his father-in-law, feasting and merry-making for several days. On the return trip to Ephraim, the Levite makes a special point of staying in an Israelite town, not a foreign town. There in Gibeah of Benjamin an old man offers him hospitality for the evening. While they eat and drink—in the formulaic expression of hospitality and feasting—base fellows surround the house and demand that the Levite be cast out to them that "they might know him" sexually. For the Israelite writer, these aggressive and violent advances are the epitome of anti-social behavior on a par with the cannibalism of the Cyclops of the Odyssey. Instead, the men offer the miscreants the Levite's woman. The evil-doers rape her, killing her. The next morning the husband finds her lying on the doorstep. In a callous and crass manner that raises issues in the ethics of gender and questions concerning the narrator's point of view in such matters, the man says, "Get up, let's go." But she is dead. The Levite cuts up the body of his wife and sends the pieces to the members of the Israelite league of allies (on scholarly debates concerning an Israelite league, see de Geus, his bibliography, and Niditch, 1982:371–74). The call is to impose justice on those who have become an abomination in Israel, committing outrageous inde-cencies, and is a visceral and shocking parallel to Saul's calling up of allies to fight the Ammonites by cutting up a yoke of oxen and sending the pieces to other Israelites with a warning that they join the fight or suffer the fate of the oxen (1 Sam 11:7). This complex tale presents important issues in sexual and family ethics and deals with various levels of human relationship: relations between spouses; between in-laws; between Israelites and non-Israelites; between anti-social Israelites and upstanding hospitable ones; and between var-ious groupings of Israelites. The complex narrative elicits questions concerning forms of social structure in ancient Israel and about its writers' assumptions about national or ethnic identity. The tale is also relevent for the study of the ban as God's justice.

As in the case of Joshua 22, the narrator does not use the "ban" term, *ḥrm*, but aspects of the tale are elucidated by the ideology of the ban as God's justice. The Hebrew text is difficult at Judg 20:9–10, but the Greek manuscript tradition reads "And now, this is the thing we will do to Gibeah; we will go up to her by lot." The casting of lots may be to determine who is guilty (cf. the Achan incident in Joshua 7). Hence the request to Benjamin at v. 13 "Give over the base fellows who are in Gibeah and we will kill them and burn out the evil from Israel." But, the casting of lots more likely refers to the means of mustering the army—ten men of a hundred as the transition from 20:9 to 20:10 seems to indicate—and not to the identification of wrong-doers (So BDB:174; Col 2; "e"). The Greek text of v. 10 implies that the battle is with Gibeah as a whole. In this case, 20:13 translated ambiguously in NRSV "Hand over those scoundrels in Gibeah," should be understood to mean that the people of Gibeah are all scoundrels, deserving of punishment. All its people have been tainted by the grave sin of the few. So Achan's entire household must suffer the consequences of his theft. Benjamin's refusal to hand over Gibeah then becomes an understandable indictment of the harsh ideology of the ban. Why should the whole city suffer for the sins of some of its members? The ban ideology is, in fact, incompatible with positive inner-group relations. As discussed in chapter 1, in most traditional societies, wars of extermination are appropriate forms of aggression only against outsiders, not within one's own group. When the ban is used as a technique to keep in-group miscreants in line by a nervous and insecure leadership with the power to enforce its will, it becomes a divisive ideology, destructive of the body politic. Implicit in the biblical ban as God's justice is the notion that the uncleanness passes from the guilty ones to the members of their family or to their town. Are the Israelites portrayed as considering Benjamin a part of their group? I think so—the group here is Israel as Judg 19:12, 20:13, and 21:2–3 strongly imply. But this Benjaminite part of the larger Israelite group also has loyalties to other Benjaminites, its closer kin. The ban-as-God's-justice ideology when applied inside the group pits one sort of unity against another and can lead to disintegration and disaster. The Benjaminites lose the battle after much killing and destruction on both sides. While the *ḥrm* term is not used, the whole city is put to the sword (Judg 20:37) in formulaic language typical of the ban and the whole of the city rises heavenward in a column of smoke (20:40). The language of v. 48 in reference to Benjamin also evokes the ban with its references to burning all the cities and "striking by the edge of the sword" "people" to "animal" to "everything there was."

The end of the tale in Judges 21 also provides a window on the potential social divisiveness of the ban as God's justice. The Israelites had sworn a pact that no one would ever give his daughter in marriage to Benjamin (21:1). The author appears to be assuming regular exogamous relations between Israelite tribes, a situation for which there is no real historical evidence. In any event, Benjamin is to be left out of the system as a further punishment of isolation for its support of Gibeah. After the war, Israel is said to regret the decision, but such an oath cannot be wiped away. Instead the Israelites crassly use the ban as a means of snaring wives for Benjamin. They inquire if any Israelite "tribe" did not join Israel against Benjamin. Again, it is not clear socio-structurally what the designation "tribe" means in such texts. Are the groupings based on kinship, lineage, geographic location? There is in fact much debate in the scholarship about the connections between such references in the literature and actual Israelite social structure at various periods (see Introduction). In any event, Jabesh-Gilead is found to be guilty of non-participation in rooting out the evil and so can be included on the list of those devoted to destruction (Judges 21:10), but in a grossly materialist and non-conforming application of the ban, virgin girls—*bĕtûlōt* "who have not known a man (sexually)"—are to be spared and taken for the Benjaminites. (21:11–12). The *bĕtûlāh* is a girl (usually of marriageable age) who has not yet married (see P.L. Day, 1989a). Men, other women, and all children are to be slaughtered (21:10–11). How debased the ban as God's justice appears in this passage and how thoroughly debased the Israelites have become in war.

Does the narrator of Judges 19–21 share my view of its lessons in political ethics concerning the ban as God's justice? Several scholars have suggested that this tale has been framed by a pro-monarchic author attempting to portray the pre-monarchic period as a time of chaos, "when there was no king in Israel and everyone did what was right in his own eyes," a frequent refrain in Judges (Lasine). If this interpretation is correct, the author of Judges 19–21 may be less sympathetic to the ideology of the ban as God's justice than the Deuteronomic writer responsible for Deuteronomy 13 and Joshua 22. What is most interesting is that in this corpus from Deuteronomy through 2 Kings we have already encountered three ideologies of war: the ban as sacrifice directed at foreigners; the ban as God's justice, directed inside or outside of Israel; and perhaps a critique of the ban as God's justice implying preference for some alternate ideology of war.

Leaders Who Employ the Ban?

Another biblical passage that does not use the ban term *ḥrm* but that has implicit connections to the ban as God's justice is 2 Kings 9–10, the story of the purge of the Omride dynasty by a man named Jehu who subsequently assumes the throne. This passage leads to the question whether the ban as God's justice was actually employed by an Israelite leader to bring about reform via war or to punish enemies.

Jehu is an army commander, encouraged by prophetic election to undertake a coup against the house of Ahab (2 Kgs 9:1–10), fulfilling Elijah's prophecy of 1 Kgs 21:20–24. Ahab who ruled the northern kingdom of Israel from 869 to 850 BCE is described as being an unethical incorrigible idolater (see 1 Kings 21), led on by his foreign, zealous, Baal-worshipping wife Jezebel, who persecuted Elijah and the other strict Yahweh worshippers. Ahab himself has already died in battle (1 Kgs 22:37) and his son Joram reigns. Jehu assassinates Joram and Jezebel as well as King Ahaziah of Judah, Joram's ally, and then strong-arms the elders of Samaria to murder all of Ahab's sons, making them accomplices in his purge. He goes on to slaughter the worshippers of Baal, putting them to the sword, none escaping (2 Kgs 10:25), *ḥērem*-style, with a warning to his men that whoever lets anyone escape will forfeit his own life (2 Kgs 10:24). "His life in place of his life" (cf. 1 Kgs 20:39). Does this verse suggest the ban as sacrifice, carried out ironically as the worshippers of Baal solemnly prepare the sacrifice to their god? The Deuteronomic view of Jehu's purge is positive (see Olyan:654); he is shown to declare himself filled with zeal for the Lord (2 Kgs 10:16; compare 2 Kgs 10:29, 31). The judgment of the eighth-century BCE Northern prophet Hosea concerning Jehu is negative; his oracle from God declares that the house of Jehu is to be punished because of the blood of Jezreel (Hos 1:4). Hosea thus accuses Jehu of blood-letting excesses, excesses which may be more the rule than the exception in crusades. Historians accept that Jehu's purge took place, but only the author of 2 Kings 9 and 10 presents the purge in terms that evoke the ideology of the ban as God's justice (contrast 2 Chron 22:7-9). This presentation may reflect shaping by the same Deuteronomic author or sort of author who produced Deuteronomy 13. One wonders if a ninth-century BCE historical figure such as Jehu was motivated by a ban ideology to undertake his coup. Did he think he was engaging in a divinely supported and demanded cleansing slaughter justified by the enemies' sins? It is difficult to know. So he is portrayed in 2 Kings 9-10. Another passage relevant in this context is 1 Sam 22:6-19. Saul takes vengeance on the priestly city Nob because of the priest Abimelech's aid of David, whom Saul accuses correctly of being a usurper of his throne. The ban nuance enters with the formulaic language of 22:19: "And Nob, city of the priests, he struck with the edge of the sword, from man to woman, child to infant, and ox, donkey, and sheep—to the sword." Did Saul think of himself as imposing a ban as God's justice against enemies of God's anointed? The Deuteronomic history in which this passage is found is markedly pro-Davidic and anti-Saulide in attitude, for Josiah is in the line of David. It is likely that a pro-Davidic writer employs the banning formula at 1 Sam 22:19 to portray Saul as using the ban in an illegal, ungodly way against God's priests. As he is accused of attempting to usurp Samuel's priestly prerogatives at 1 Sam 13:9-14, here he is portrayed as using the ban unjustly to exterminate political opponents, but does not such a banning mentality almost inevitably lead to this sort of thing if it is part of the guiding ideology of those with the power to use force to impose their will?

History and the Ban as God's Justice

Was the ideology of the ban as God's justice ever enacted by an Israelite ruler to come to power or keep power? The cases of Jehu and Saul offer the possibility that some Israelites interpreted the ban in terms of God's justice hundreds of years before the Josianic reform and the Deuteronomic shaping of the corpus from Deuteronomy through 2 Kings.

I would like to agree with Norman Gottwald's comments on a more broadly defined ideology "holy war," which for Gottwald describes texts in both of my ban trajectories: ". . . holy war as stated in the Deuteronomic history was actually a *theoretical* [my italics] dogma" (Gottwald, 1964:307; see also Weinfeld, 1972:167). And yet, are biblical Israelites of a crusading persuasion so different from later Christian actualizers? If Israelites who believe in the ideology of the ban as God's justice have the means to impose their will, will they not invoke the ban? What does such a "dogma" offer its adherents? In the Hebrew Scriptures, the ban as God's justice is an ideology of those who consider themselves disempowered and beset, politically, economically, and culturally.

Philip Stern considers the ban always to have been associated in Israelite world-view with the condemnation of idolatry (1989:156; 1991:104), so that his work should be mentioned under the heading of wars for which are made claims of God's justice, but Stern reaches a conclusion quite different from the one offered here concerning those who might espouse the ideology of the ban as God's justice. He views the tone of Deuteronomy 20, for example, as confident and "not from the end of the 7th century declining Southern (Judean) Kingdom, but from the heyday of the North" (1989:148; see also 1991:98), that is of the Northern Kingdom ruled by non-Davidic kings from the time of Jeroboam to its conquest by Assyria in 721 BCE. His "working hypothesis" is that the traditions behind the *ḥērem* texts in Deuteronomy and Joshua stem from "a time when the North was of sufficient power to contemplate the use of the *ḥērem* itself" (1989:131, also 172; 1991:89).

Quite to the contrary, the ban-as-God's-justice ideology is a way in which a group that fears loss of its identity attempts to define itself. This ideology is characterized by a put-the-wagons-in-a-circle mentality that David Little has referred to as "communalism" (1989:8), the world-view of a group not only distrustful of foreigners but of "foreigners" in its own midst, enemies among former brethren. It is this sort of mentality that Girard describes for groups who seek a scapegoat, this sort of world-view that Louis Stulman, following on the work of von Rad (1953:58–59) describes for the

Deuteronomic tradition (D). "The world of D is fragile and fraught with danger, and Israel's survival is perceived to be in jeopardy. . . . Chaotic social forces—enemies, criminals, and indigenous outsiders—threaten to undermine its social and cosmic order . . ." (Stulman:626). Defining the "Other" deserving of destruction is a means of asserting and of creating a self worthy of preservation.

Brekelmans is linear and evolutionary in his treatment of the ban whereas this study suggests that various ideologies of the ban and of war existed contemporaneously in Israelite culture. In his trajectory, pre-Deuteronomic northern reformers, playing roles much like Samuel in 1 Samuel 15 and the unnamed prophet in 1 Kings 20, reinterpret an earlier version of the ban involving the war-vow in terms of sin and judgment (1959b; see also Rofé, 1985:24–26). That the ideology of the ban as God's justice pre-dates the Josianic period is certainly possible as noted above, but the full flowering of this ideology of war is to be understood, I believe, in the background to the Josianic reform.

During the reign of Josiah's immediate predecessor, Manasseh, the southern kingdom Judeah had been totally subservient politically and economically to the super-power Assyria, the Northern kingdom Israel having been overthrown by Assyria in 721 BCE. The reformers who would take power under Manasseh's grandson Josiah describe life under Manasseh as one of cultural and religious deprivation.

> He rebuilt the high places that his father Hezekiah had destroyed. He erected altars to Baal and made an Ashera as Ahab, King of Israel, had done. They bowed down to all the host of heaven and worshipped them (2 Kgs 21:3). He built altars to all the host of heaven in the two courts of the house of the Lord and he made his son pass through the fire. He practiced soothsaying and divination and appointed spirit mediums and wizards. He did so much evil in the eyes of the Lord that he incited him to anger. He put a carved image of Ashera that he made in the house about which Yahweh had said to David and Solomon, his son, "In this house and in Jerusalem, which I have chosen from all the tribes of Israel, I will set my name forever" (2 Kgs 21:5-7).

Manasseh is thus accused of encouraging polytheism, idolatry, wizardry, and child sacrifice all under the influence of Assyrian

culture and religion. The reformers, themselves no doubt person-
ally persecuted as rebels and subversives by forces more willing to
accommodate the Assyrian presence in the region, long for the day
of vengeance, a day when "pure Yahwism" (a creation of their
minds and never a reality in history in Israel) could be restored, and
they blame political and economic difficulties not on Assyria but on
the disobedience of their own ancestors doomed to punishment by
God (2 Kgs 22:13). The Assyrian Empire itself falls, Nineveh the
capital being destroyed in 612 BCE, giving the reformers their
chance. Manasseh's son Amon is killed in a coup by these forces,
and his eight-year-old son Josiah is crowned king under the watch-
ful eye of the high priest Hilkiah, a member of the reform group.

If there is any period in which the dogma of the ban as God's
justice became a reality it should have been during the reign of
Josiah, who conducted various purges of those regarded as idolators (e.g. 2 Kgs 23:20). It is interesting that the term $ḥrm$ or
technical language associated with the ban is not found in 2 Kings
23, the chapter devoted to describing Josiah's reform. Could it be
that cooler heads prevail once a monarchy sympathetic to the
reformers takes over? Or has the harsh reality of the reformers'
crusade been sanitized by later authors' abbreviated reports? The
Deuteronomic writers, in any event, shape the banning traditions of
the biblical conquest theme in terms of matters of convenantal
justice. And in Deuteronomy 13, they make clear that the ban as
God's justice is not only to be invoked against foreigners, but also
to deal with those whom Louis Stulman calls "the indigenous
other," the enemy within. In a similar fashion, the classical prophets
believed that God's vengeance could be turned not only against
Israel's enemies, but also against Israel herself to punish her for
breaking covenant (Am 2:4–16; 5:1–27; see also Isa 43:28).

In the process, the reformers put the ban on a different theoretical basis than the notion that God accepts human sacrifice, an idea
anathema to them. The ban as God's justice would have appealed to
post-Josianic, exilic, and post-exilic writers in the Deuteronomic
tradition as well, a reminder that foreign conquerors who are by
definition unlawful and unjust will be defeated eventually like the
Ammorites of olden days. The ban, moreover, self-righteously
guards against the sixth-century BCE members of their own com-

munity who might not share their vision of a pure restored Israel after the fall of Babylon, the super-power that follows Assyria.

Guilt, Killing, Kin, Purity: The Ban as Sacrifice versus the Ban as God's Justice

It is not easy for humans to kill others. To participate in mass killing in war is destructive of individual psyches and of the larger community's mental health. The ban in either trajectory is a means of making killing in war acceptable. How do the ban as sacrifice and the ban as God's justice differ in this regard? The ban as sacrifice is a part of war against those who are not of one's group, a means of securing God's aid in victory. The ban sometimes has to be imposed to win. God demands his portion and cannot be refused. The reasoning goes "If we offer them, we may be saved." Group solidarity is thus increased—better we should live than they—and guilt is reduced—God demands his offerings—but the enemy is recognized as human, worthy of God's sacrifice. Inanimate booty can almost always be kept, because God has received the best portion. In contrast, the ban-as-God's-justice ideology actually motivates and encourages war, implying that wars of extermination are desirable in order to purify the body politic of one's own group, to eradicate evil in the world beyond one's group, and to actualize divine judgment. In the ban as God's justice a sharp line is drawn between us and them, between clean and unclean, between those worthy of salvation and those deserving elimination. The enemy is thus not a mere human, an offering, necessary to win the assistance of God, but a monster, unclean, and diseased. The ban as God's justice thus allows people to accept the notion of killing other humans by dehumanizing them and the process of dehumanization can take place even within the group during times of stress, distrust, and anomie.

3

The Priestly Ideology of War
in Numbers 31

Numbers 31 is an intriguing and neglected biblical text with which
scholars often confess frustration. One scholar calls the passage
"Midrash" and appears to use the term disparagingly (Gray: 417–
19) while another admits that "it is not easy to make out what the
real subject-matter of this long section is supposed to be" (Noth
1968:228).

Numbers 31 is usually discussed as an example of a banning text,
but its ideology of war differs from the ban as sacrifice and the ban
as God's justice in important and intriguing ways that identify a
world-view different from those explored thus far.

Within the biblical odyssey of the people Israel, Numbers 31 is
set near the end of the period of desert wanderings, before the death
of Moses.

War and Vengeance

The passage begins with God's command to Moses, "Avenge the
Israelites upon the Midianites for afterwards you will be gathered
to your people." The author thus claims just cause for war, but
what did Midian do? They had hired the diviner Balaam to curse
Israel (Num 22:7), and he, in fact, dies in just revenge at Num 31:8,

killed by sword along with the Midianite kings (on Balaam's death see Olson:161). And the Midianite women had enticed Israelites to idolatry in the incident at Baal Peor (Num 25:6, 14–18), a matter also alluded to at 31:16. Note again that Balaam is implicated. Numbers 31 thus might be regarded as the inclusio for Numbers 25. While chapter 25 describes the people's idolatry, chapter 31 provides the necessary catharsis and the possibility to atone for that act of infidelity to God (So Olson).

Attitudes to Midianites and to Balaam vary in the Hebrew Scriptures. Moses is given Midianite connections at Ex 2:15; his father-in-law Jethro is described respectfully as "a priest of Midian" (2:16). Scholars have seen in pro- and anti-Midian passages material preserved by pro-Moses or anti-Moses priestly groups who claim descent by Moses and Aaron respectively. Whether or not ancient Mushite versus Aaronid rivalries are revealed by these texts, contrasting in attitudes to Midianites, it is clear that in its current form Numbers 31 has a strongly anti-Midianite bent; indeed the enemy is the "Other" not deserving of pity. So Balaam, who is an interesting, even comical, itinerant prophet-for-hire in the story of Numbers 22–24, is here, as in later Rabbinic tradition, turned into an arch-villain. In one narrative thread in the tale of Num 22–24, he communicates with Yahweh and recognizes God's power over him (22:8–12, 18–21), while in another he, like a Jonah, tries to get around God's word in order to accommodate his paying customers (22:21–22). He has nothing to do with the events at Peor (chapter 25), nor is the role of the Midianites clear in this textually difficult chapter (see 25:1–2, 6, 16–18) in which v. 18 is an attempt to neaten things up.

Numbers 31, however, is strongly marked by an us-them attitude to these non-Israelites. Important in conveying this distrust of "them" in Numbers 25 and 31 is the portrayal of alien women as sensuous and evil enticers, embodiments of the wrong way, the foreign way, the way of idolatry and anti-Yahwism (Num 25:1, 6–8, 15, 18). This web of ensnarement issues forth also from the "strange woman" of Proverbs 1–9 (Camp). Terms of deception and trickery are applied to the Midianites (Num 25:18) while the Midianite woman specifically implicated at Num 25:6 is, in fact, named Cozbi, a name meant to play on the root *kzb* meaning to lie or be deceptive. Num 31:16 dredges up the theme of entrapment by the

Midianite women and links it to Balaam, suggesting that the women had acted on his advice.

Perhaps the writers of Numbers 31 are Aaronid priests still fighting the old battles against the Midianite connections of Moses. Numbers 31 is priestly literature of some sort—few would doubt it (Gray:419; Budd:328-29)—but the theme, as we will see below, is more sweeping than a matter of honor due ancient priestly houses. The authors are anxious to discount any connections with foreigners found in the tradition. They wish to leave no doubt about the worthiness of Balaam or the loyalty of Midianites. They are portrayed as evil, deserving of eradication, and Israel is a pristine entity to be kept apart from them. The emphasis in Numbers 31 on providing reasons for the enemies' elimination is marked: They had hired a male wizard to curse Israel, while the Midianite women had cast their own spell, seducing Israel into apostasy. It is not enough to say as in the ban as sacrifice that certain enemies simply must be destroyed as "banned" (e.g., Josh 6:17-21; 8:1-2). Here as in Deuteronomic passages treating the ban as God's justice, the crusade has to be shown to be just and deserved. At Num 31:3 Moses tells people they are to deliver "the vengeance of the Lord" to Midian. The same idiom is found in Jeremiah 50:15, 28 and 51:11 in which, as in Numbers 31, war is described as necessary and justified, for the enemies, the Babylonians, are plunderers (50:11) and sinners (50:14) (see chapter 2 above). Israel is to do to Babylon what Babylon has done to them (50:15). This is just vengeance for God's temple (NRSV) which the Babylonians had destroyed or the vengeance of the divine palace (50:28), a God-sent act of war. Jer 51:3-11 makes the link between the ban and the Lord's vengeance explicit. "Do not spare her young men, place her whole host (or army) under the ban (51:3b). . . . for it is the vengeance of the Lord, vengeance for his temple" (51:11). The words "spare" and "ban" exist in a contrastive and technical relationship in the tradition. When one does not totally "ban," one "has compassion" or "spares" as in the directions to Saul concerning what *not* to do with Agag, directions ignored by the king (1 Sam 15:3, 9; see also 1 Sam 15:15; Deut 13:8 [v. 9 in Hebrew]). For Jeremiah, this ban equals God's vengeance: it is total, unsparing, on God's behalf, ordered by God for a holy cause, and justified by vengeance.

Placing under the Ban and Numbers 31:
Revealing Differences

Numbers 31 does not use the root *hrm* (ban) and does not like Jeremiah go the step further to associate "vengeance of the Lord" with that term. On the other hand, in seeking to understand Numbers 31 in terms of the other war texts of the Hebrew Bible, it is to a comparison with passages containing the ban as God's justice that one is drawn. Like these texts, Numbers 31 involves divinely commanded wars and as in Deut 20:2–4 a priestly role; the "kill" term found in Num 31:7,8 is language associated with the ban at Joshua 8:24,26 and figures prominently in the Moabite Mesha Inscription (Stern, 1989:61); and the image of killing with the sword found in Num 31:8 is also expressed in typical ban language. The enemies' towns and encampments are "burned with fire" (Num 31:10), again a phrase and a phenomenon typical of biblical ban texts. And ultimately, once Moses has his way, almost all of the enemy is slain as in ban texts, but not *all* of the enemy. The nature of the incompleteness of the killing is a key to understanding the distinctive war ideology of Numbers 31.

As discussed in previous chapters the primary and most consistent characteristic of texts that employ ban language is neither strafing cities by fire, nor the total destruction of the enemies' goods. Though these are frequent accompanying aspects of the ban especially in the most extremist descriptions, the most constant feature of the ban is the annihilation of all human life regardless of age, gender, or military status.

In some senses Moses is put in a position typical of spiritual leaders of holy wars in the Bible. As Samuel does with Saul in a passage dominated by the ideology of the ban as God's justice (1 Sam 15:10–23) and the anonymous prophet with Ahab in a passage dominated by the ban as sacrifice (1 Kgs 20:42), he chastises the people/king for not prosecuting the war with adequate zeal and completeness. The completeness in this case does not require that all booty be given up; after purification, booty is to be carefully apportioned among God, Levites, soldiers, and the people. Nor is he angry that a king or kings have been spared, for they have all been slain (Num 31:8; cf 1 Sam 15:9, 19–23). Rather, not enough people have been killed, for the children and women have been spared (Num 31:9) along with cattle, flocks, and goods. Had Moses insisted that all humans be killed, the passage would be classifiable in terms of a ban ideology, but Moses allows that virgin girls be spared, thereby setting this passage apart from the vast majority of ban texts. Several questions present themselves. Why should virgin girls be spared? How does Moses justify killing the rest? What does the sparing of the girls reveal about the ways in which the author of Numbers 31 symbolically orders reality and about attitudes to gender in his world? Where does this text stand in an inner biblical spectrum of war ideologies? If not the ban, what?

The brief stutter at Num 31:15–16 and Num 31:17 is interesting. On the one hand, as in Jeremiah 50–51, justification is given for the wholesale taking of life. The sexually active women deserve to die, for they had enticed Israel to sin at Baal Peor. As discussed above, this text and Num 25:16–18 put a particular anti-Midianite spin on the incident described at Numbers 25:1–3. In any event, as in Deut 20:18 a reason is given for wiping out the enemy: they entice Israel to worship other gods. Not only might Midianite women come to entice Israel, they are already guilty of doing so. (On biblical holy war and divine judgment see Good.) But what of 31:17 demanding that all male children be killed? No justification is given for the killing of little boys.

A Strongly Hierarchical Vision of War

In contrast to the melees in the Book of Joshua, the battle in Numbers 31 is imagined to be fought by large organized armies, within a clearly stratified society of priests, commanders, soldiers, and citizens. This is an imagining of war that has more in common with the priestly, apocalyptic Qumran War Scroll of the first century BCE than with descriptions of the conquest in the Deuteronomic History. The description of the distribution of booty after the war has the precision and list-making quality of the directions for offerings in Ezek 45:13–17 and for land apportionment in Ezekiel 48 (passages of the sixth century BCE) in contrast to the briefer, one-line accounts following Joshua's battles (e.g. Josh 8:27).

We cite these differences not to make the case that the ban texts in Joshua or elsewhere in the Deuteronomic History are pre-monarchic and early. In dealing with the ban as sacrifice and the ban as God's justice, matters of chronology have been dealt with more complexly by tracing trajectories of ideology. It does seem clear, however, that the writer of Numbers 31 is fully at home in a sophisticated political outlook that has experienced monarchy. In fact, the world-view underlying this text is post-monarchic and priestly.

The priest is not merely the pre-battle homilist, as in Deut 20:2-4, or the one who helps to remove from the troops those who might be distracted by personal matters, thereby also reducing the size of the armed forces so that God's role as victor in holy war becomes all the clearer. The priest is rather the leader of the armed forces, collected in orderly round numbers, a thousand from each tribe. The priest leads this substantial army with symbols of his status, temple vessels and special trumpets, which only priests are allowed to make and use (Num 10:2, 7-10; cf. 2 Chron 13:12; Neh 12:35; 1 Chron 15:24, 16:6; 2 Chron 5:12, 13). One out of every fifty items of spoil—be they people or animals—goes to the Levites and much also to the control of Eleazar the priest for an offering to the Lord.

This portrayal of war stems from a post-monarchic, late-biblical priestly writer who departs from both the ban ideologies in the important respect that the lives of some human beings, virginal girls, are spared. But, if these are politically sophisticated texts, why is not more human spoil utilized? As Bainton muses (46), why waste people? The answer so far is theological and perceived in terms of divine judgment. Those who entice to foreign worship deserve to die. This explanation does not explain, however, why girl children are spared and not boys. The sparing of girls is clearly not a matter of just war, an ethical concern to save the guiltless. While 31:15-16 appeals to just cause to explain the killing of women, v. 17 erases the mirage.

Women as Chattel, Issues of Purity:
Judges 21, Deuteronomy 21, and Numbers 31

One might again appeal to ecological, biological, and economic explanations for the sparing of virgin girls. While a group may not have the means to control an adult male slave labor force, societies in which women die young, often in childbirth, may well have use for more women to serve as wives and to produce children to work (Vayda, 1967:87; Davie 1929:89–102; Meyers: 70–71). On the other hand, why not suggest taking all the children if the labor force is imagined able to use them—they are young, pliant, and trainable. That is what the Bantu do when they fight non-Bantu (Wager:228). Why not take all women of child-bearing age? In many cultures— cultural being synonymous with androcentric—the women along with cattle and other spoil are the trophies of war, chattel to be conquered from the enemy people, i.e. its men. This sort of assumption about conquered women is, in fact, reflected in Deut 20:14, Deut 21:10–14, Gen 34:29, and 2 Kgs 5:2. Laban is portrayed accusing Jacob of disloyalty and impropriety at Gen 31:26 by saying, "You have deceived me by leading away my daughters like captives of the sword." Women are war-spoils, often catalogued with cattle and moveable possessions (Deut 20:14). The notion of men as people and women as something other than full people is at play in Numbers 31, but even more central in defining the status of conquered women are issues of purity.

One other war text in the Hebrew Bible that in contrast to Numbers 31 directly employs the language of the ban also allows for—in fact, requires—the saving of young girls and for overtly expressed reasons involving the need for wives.

As discussed in chapter 2, the Benjaminites have refused to participate in a holy war against Gibeah, some of whose citizens raped and murdered a woman staying with her husband overnight in the city. This disgraceful crime is cause for united Israelite action to root out the evil in their midst, just cause for the sort of war described in Deuteronomy 13. But Benjamin will not join Israel to fight its tribal kin from Gibeah and so a terrible civil war ensues. The Israelites vow to punish Benjamin by isolation; they will not give their daughters in marriage to the men of that tribe, but after the war regret what they now regard as having been too harsh a penalty. And so in a crass and Machiavellian use of the ban ideology, they ask if any from the tribes of Israel had failed to join in the just crusade against Benjamin. Sure enough, they find that the residents of Jabesh–Gilead had not participated and use this as an excuse to kill all the people under the ban, sparing only the young girls "who had not yet known a man" sexually and they give the women children to the Benjaminites for wives. These females not being numerous enough, however, they discard all pretense of just cause and instruct the Benjaminites simply to steal additional women from Shiloh.

Both Numbers 31 and Judges 21 reflect the male, patriarchal biological interest in purity of line, of seed. No man can ever be sure of who his father is, nor a conquering male that a non-virgin captive's child is his own. This is a culture in which the biological, visceral link to children must be certain, a hint that it is a culture, like that of Ezra, very nervous about its identity and self-definition. There are, of course, ways to deal with fears about the purity of line, such as a waiting period of several months before the man lies with the woman, but neither Numbers 31 nor Judges 21 reflects measured patience. Their treatment of the women is brutal and brief. In Numbers 31, however, matters of virginity and attitudes to women are interwoven with a more complex web of purity concerns.

Deut 21:10–14 allows the captive woman a certain identity as belonging to the enemy, and requires a rite of passage that will change the woman from one of "them" to one of "us." Thus her head is shaven, her nails pared, her clothing exchanged. While Deut 21:10–14 does not mention virginity directly, the captured woman is pictured as a virgin bride, allowed a month to "weep over" the loss of her father and mother. There is an assumption that a virgin woman can be altered like clothing. Once she has sex, however, she becomes unalterable, marked or branded by her husband's "personness." Thus Deut 21:14 insists that the Israelite husband is in some way responsible for the female captive he has raped. She cannot be sold like a slave. His person and hers have become interwoven through sexual contact. The woman, moreover, can transmit the man's essence to another man who lies with her, while for his part, he absorbs her essence. It is not lightly that the tradition in Genesis 2 describes man and woman as becoming one flesh, nor surprising that men become unclean by having intercourse with a woman who is unclean (Lev 15:24). It is understandable in this system of symbols that a priest must marry a virgin who is to be filled with his holiness alone (Lev 21:7). While Deut 21:11 allows that the captive be a mature virgin woman—she is called "woman" and not "child"—Numbers 31 puts her age further back to make the fence around her purity stronger and I believe to have her "unmarked," blank-slate quality all the clearer. [Contrast Milgrom (1990:259) who would translate "young woman" influenced by Num 14:29–31.] Here we have the explanation as to why young boys are not spared. In Judges 21, only female children are saved because the raid is precisely to capture wives for Benjamin, the purer and the newer, the better. But in Numbers 31 the distinction between male children and female children is made very clear in the context of a map marked "us versus them," pure versus impure. The antagonistic emotions of war intertwine with purity regulations. As noted above, us-them attitudes in Numbers 31 are very strong in the portrayal of Midian. The enemy is to be killed, wiped out. Little boys grow up to be warriors and are perhaps killed for that reason, but more important, little boys are small men who are markedly "the enemy" and sexually active women have been marked by the enemy and are of a piece with them. They convey the uncleanness of the seductive female idolator, a capacity to pollute that is switched on only by their active sexuality. Only those who have no identity, who are truly clean slates, are spared—the virgin girl children. This priestly attitude to killing in war differs significantly from banning texts in which all life is to be destroyed, sometimes even including domestic animals, and has a different symbolic map.

War and Purity: Contrast between Ban Texts and Numbers 31

In passages reflecting the ideology of the ban as God's justice, the enemy is the "Other," unclean, and the destruction sometimes includes even the objects the unclean ones have touched (Josh 7:24–26). In ban texts in which booty can be taken, it is assumed to be de facto clean. In Numbers 31 finer distinctions are made between animate and inanimate booty and between those humans who are markedly "Other" and those who are less clearly marked, and so sparable. Greater care, moreover, is taken in purifying both that which is captured and those who fought.

All spoil that can be spared must be made clean. The captured women children are to remain outside the camp and be purified on the priestly, holy, prime-number third and seventh days (31:19). Every garment, every article of skin, everything made of goat's hair, and every article of wood is to be purified (31:20). As for the booty, that which can withstand fire is to be purified with fire and then with the water of purification, that which cannot stand the fire is to be purified with water (31:23). (On the various modes of purification in Numbers 31 and connections with Num 19:10–20 see D.P. Wright.) After seven days the prisoners are to wash their clothes and return to camp. The seven-day unclean period is familiar from other priestly prescriptions (e.g. Lev 13:31 on skin diseases; Lev 15:13 on discharges; Lev 15:19,28 on menstruation and irregular bleeding). The need to transform or cleanse captured people has already been discussed for Deut 21:12–13. Different here is the need to cleanse the inanimate objects and animal booty. The uncleanness of the enemy "Other" has attached to them and perhaps also the uncleanness of death, for in Numbers killing in battle is unclean-rendering.

The warriors themselves who have killed or touched a corpse must stay outside the camp for a week with their captives and be purified (31:19). Generally in Leviticus, contact with corpses is not defiling, nor is blood from a wound (but on carcasses even of kosher animals see Lev 11:39). Priests become unclean from touching a corpse (Lev 21:1, 2, 11) and are to avoid the dead as much as possible. In Num 5:1–4 the uncleanness-rendering capacity of a human corpse extends to all Israelites in the context of the "camp," perhaps reflecting the status of the people as holy warriors. Numbers 19:10–13, however, generalizes this uncleanness rule as "a perpetual statute for the people of Israel and for the alien who dwells among them." Anyone who touches any dead human is rendered unclean. As in Numbers 31, he must be purified with water on the third and seventh days (19:12; see also 19:16 and purification by sprinkling, washing, and bathing at 19:17–19; for a discussion of varying biblical traditions concerning corpse uncleanness see Milgrom 1978:515–16; 1981). Thus for the tradition in Numbers, war necessarily is a defiling activity. To consider war defiling, albeit in the context of a world-view that divides the world into clean and unclean, nevertheless is an ethical perception of sorts. The enemy is after all human; the shedding of human blood tears the whole fabric of the cosmos and must be duly marked off, separated from mundane experience (See Wenham:212). It is some reflection of this attitude to war that one finds in 1 Chronicles' explanation for David's not building the temple in Jerusalem. As a warrior, he had shed too much blood to be allowed to build the holy house where God will allow his spirit to dwell on earth (1 Chron 28:3).

And yet it is a priest, son of the High Priest, who leads the people to war armed with sacred trumpets and holy vessels, accoutrements of that holy place in Numbers 31. The leadership presence of the priest and symbols of his office mark this text as priestly literature. *kĕlê haqqōdeš*, "holy vessels," are mentioned rather than *kĕlê milḥāmāh*, "instruments of war." Are the holy vessels, in fact, symbols of the soldiers' purity, that they come to war with clean hands and hearts? At 1 Sam 21:4–5 (vv. 5–6 in the Hebrew) David tells the priest of Nob that his men are entitled to partake of sacred loaves because they have stayed away from women: "The vessels of the young men are holy." Their persons are clean and unpolluted by sexual contact with women. They are in a state of ritual purity necessary for sacrifice and for holy war. In Numbers 31, as in Deuteronomy 20, war on some level is ritual, and yet war in Numbers 31 is not cleansing or whole-making in the spirit of the extirpation of wayward Israelite cities in Deuteronomy 13 or the ban texts demanding erasure of the idolaters from the land. Doubts have crept in about the whole enterprise, for in killing one becomes part of the abomination, the enemy one seeks to eliminate. Such are the complexities of the priestly ethics of violence in war found in Numbers 31. Is it in recognition of this ambivalence that the commanders are pictured to offer up what each has found among the personal effects of the dead enemies—articles of gold, armlets and bracelets, signet rings, earrings, and pendants—"to make atonement for ourselves before the Lord." For what do they atone? Is it for sins in general, is it finally to close the matter of Baal Peor (Olson:88), or is it to atone for the defilement of bringing death to human beings (Wenham:212; de Vaulx, 359)?

Conclusions

The study of Numbers 31 leads to fascinating questions about the psychology and ethics of violence and about images of woman as seducer and virgin. We have explored some of the ways in which a particular group in Israel sought to justify killing and not killing in war. In the process we have come to understand better a priestly symbolic world in which all is perceived in terms of clean versus unclean and us versus them, but in which the woman who has not known a man is not yet defined as belonging to one category or the other. It is the man who establishes her identity and status. Depending on her sexual status as non-virgin or virgin, the foreign woman is a seducer whose idolatrous appeals are just cause for war or a marriageable war-spoil whose entry into Israel signals the end of conflict. Finally, Numbers 31 expresses genuine ambivalence concerning the ethics of war. The cause is holy, the war is ritualized, but the killing defiles. Thus as one enters war ritually one must exit with separation, cleansing, and sacrifices of atonement.

4

The Bardic Tradition of War

Alongside the two types of ban texts in Hebrew Scriptures are threads of material, betokening views of war quite different from either ideology of the ban or the priestly ideology of Numbers 31. For the student of the Bible as traditional literature, the most interesting of these threads involves the interaction between groups of heroes, often called "mighty men," and an apparent chivalric code of conduct in regard to war. The heroes are sometimes bound by kinship relations; their battles display traits of a form of fighting Q. Wright and others have called "the duel"; accompanying the duel is a stylized feature of fighting behavior, "the taunt."

War as Part of a Literary Pattern

In the Hebrew Bible, the heroic warring material is part of larger narrative patterns that are typical of a cross-cultural range of epic stories about heroes. The life story of David is fullest in this regard including the duel with Goliath that leads to David's being taken into the inner circle of the king (1 Sam 17:1–54); the requirement that he obtain a hundred foreskins in order to receive the prize of the king's daughter in marriage, that is, the test of the would-be son-in-law of the king (1 Sam 18:24–27; cf. Josh 15:16; Judges 1:12); David's career as crafty bandit chief who attracts around him "men of valor" (2 Sam 23:8–39; 1 Chron 11–12; 2 Sam 21:18–22; 1 Chron 20:4–8); his accession to the throne; his own conquests and exploits as king; and finally his decline. War portrayals touch upon each of these narrative steps in a larger life story of the hero. The narrative steps or motifs and the warring aspects of them also appear in more isolated references in Judges, 1 and 2 Samuel, and 1 and 2 Kings, sometimes retold or reshaped in 1 and 2 Chronicles.

"Men of Valor"

The bold warriors such as Gideon, David, and his men are called "men of valor" (e.g. Judg 6:12; 1 Sam 16:18; 1 Sam 14:52; 2 Sam 17:10, 23:20, 24:9). Sometimes skill with special weapons is attributed to them (e.g. 2 Sam 24:9; 1 Chron 12:8, 8:40; 2 Chron 14:8 [v. 7 in the Hebrew]) and they appear to be a special group of Israelites, remembered as a warrior's guild of sorts (see 2 Kgs 24:14, 16). In a tradition in 1 and 2 Chronicles, the phrase "men of valor" or "mighty men" is associated with heads of "ancestral houses" or lineages; this tradition may be assuming the existence of a warrior's caste whose members are not necessarily warriors or the phrase "mighty men" may in this late biblical tradition refer to men of social, political, and economic power. (For a full discussion see Kampen:95–144.) It is the mighty men described in the bardic-style literature of the Bible that interest us here.

We are told, for example, of the exploits of Beniah, son of Jehoiada (2 Sam 23:20–23; 1 Chron 11:22–25), son of an *'îš hayil*, the epithet meaning "mighty man" or "valiant man," *rab pĕ'ālîm*, a doer of great deeds. In a brief snippet reminiscent of one-on-one battle scenes or cameos in the *Iliad*, Beniah is said to have killed an Egyptian, a handsome man (2 Sam 23:21) or a man of stature, five cubits tall (1 Chron 11:23).

> In the hand of the Egyptian was a spear, but he swooped upon him with a staff, tore the spear from the Egyptian's hand and killed him with his own spear (2 Sam 23:21).

The account of Beniah's deeds in 2 Samuel 23 also mentions other victories.

> He killed the two [sons of (LXX)] Ariel of Moab and swooped down and killed the lion in the pit on the day of the snow (2 Sam 23:20).

The use of articles in 2 Sam 23:20 is marked syntax: *the* lion, *the* pit, *the* day of the snow, implying that the author refers to a well-known tale—the one about the lion, etc. The second half of v. 20 referring to this episode is veritably poetic in its rhythms and balance, its repetitions of sounds. This together with the briefer variant in 1 Chronicles is the stuff an oral epic tradition is made of.

Similarly, one of David's men Elhanan is described as fighting Goliath, and the shaft of his spear was like a weaver's beam (2 Sam 21:19). In this case, the battle with Goliath is attributed to a hero other than David while the weapon is formulaically described in the same terms found at 1 Chron 11:23 (but not at 2 Sam 23:21) to describe the spear of the Egyptian. Another enemy is catalogued at 2 Sam 21:20 (1 Chron 20:6) as a huge man who had six fingers per hand and six toes per foot, descended from a strange race of beings called Rapha, usually translated "giants" but apparently related to the term *rĕpā'îm* meaning "shades," or "ghosts"—the extinct ones. Jonathan, son of David's brother Shimei, kills this creature after he, like Goliath, "taunts" Israel.

Taunts

The term "to taunt" is an important one in the war texts of bardic literature and is associated with the one-on-one combats typical of this thread of war portrayals. The ritualistic behavior of taunting and revenge are associated in actual duels as a form of combat in various traditional cultures (Q. Wright:1401–15). Wright shows that the goal in taunting is, in fact, to preserve prestige and avoid physical combat: the taunt is often accompanied by bluffing, counter-taunting, and more bluffing. In 2 Sam 21:21, however, the taunt as challenge is met and the one who initiated the power struggle is countered with deadly force. An Israelite taunts the Philistines at 2 Sam 23:9, and singlehandedly makes good on his verbal assassination of the enemy (2 Sam 23:9–10). So the tribe Zebulun is described poetically at Judges 5:18 as taunting death himself (see also 2 Kgs 19:23 = Isa 37:23; Zeph 2:8–10). In an inner Israelite power struggle, Gideon accuses the people of Succoth of having taunted him (Judg 8:14) of being unable to capture Zebah and Zalmuna, the kings of Midian. In this related expansion of the duel situation, they challenge his manhood and power. He must prove himself and take vengeance. He does capture the kings and takes vengeance on Succoth as he had sworn he would (Judg 8:7, 16–17).

Taunting and the Battle with Goliath

Taunting as part of a duel scene is especially prominent in the combat between Goliath and David at 1 Samuel 17. Goliath is described in detail in 17:4–7, his height, his armor, his spear—again like a weaver's beam. His taunt (17:8–10) challenges Israel to provide a suitable single combatant to fight with him and decide the winner of the day's battle. Again the one-on-one duel is found in the midst of the larger war. Drama is high and the concept of war as sport or contest is prevalent, as is the concern with prestige (cf. Vermeule:85). David asks "Who is this uncircumcised Philistine who would taunt the ranks of the living God?" David also asks "What will be done for the man who kills that Philistine and removes the taunt from upon Israel?" (17:26). A taunt is a challenge, a dare that cannot be ignored unless the object of the challenge and implicit insult wishes to admit cowardice, womanishness, and defeat. To meet the challenge and remove the taunt is to obtain status and glory. The man who removes the taunt will receive riches, the king's daughter, and the status of freemen for the members of his father's household (1 Sam 17:25). (See de Vaux, 1966:123.) David is very interested in the reward for defeating Goliath (17:26). Broader issues of the warrior's status and pride for his group intertwine with the specific traditional narrative about David's status as hero on the rise.

When Goliath and David meet, they exchange insults worthy of the taunting situation of the duel.

> The Philistine looked, saw David, and regarded him with contempt because he was a young lad, ruddy and handsome. The Philistine said to David, "Am I a dog that you come to me with sticks?" and the Philistine cursed David in the name of his gods. The Philistine said to David "Come against me and I will feed your flesh to the birds of the sky and the beasts of the field" (1 Sam 17:42–44).

Goliath attempts to put David in his place, to gain the psychological advantage by implying David has no chance against him, that it is an insult even to face such an opponent in combat (cf. Vermeule:99, 101). Goliath also implies that the warrior deserves to be met by his equal—a role the inexperienced David does not appear to suit. This is an aspect of a warrior's code we will encounter repeatedly (cf. the encounters between Asahel and Abner and between Gideon and the Midianite kings below). Goliath describes in gory detail what his enemy can expect in defeat while the Israelite narrator already erases Goliath by referring to him repeatedly not by name, but simply as "the Philistine." For his part, David boasts that he has killed lions and bears and that Goliath will die like them for having dared to taunt the ranks of the living God (1 Sam 17:36). The Israelite author's religious orientation shapes the warrior's boasts as David emphasizes God's role in his victory. He repeats the threat to Goliath that Goliath had directed at him—that Philistine corpses will become food for the birds and beasts—in the very same language used by Goliath (1 Sam 17:44, 46). We should not forget that Goliath had counted on his gods as well (17:43) (McCarter, 1984:98). When David defeats Goliath, it is a victory for the young warrior, the Israelites, and Yahweh.

War as Sport

Another war portrayal that imagines a man-to-man contest as a pause in the larger war is found at 2 Sam 2:12-16. The very language of this text emphasizes the "sporting" aspect of combat noted earlier. The larger conflict is the civil war between the forces supporting Saul's kingship and those supporting the insurgency of David. The generals, Abner and Joab, and their men are described as sitting on opposite sides of the pool of Gibeon (2 Sam 2:13). Abner, Saul's general, proposes a contest between selected men of each side—the idiom is literally "let the lads rise up and make sport before us." And Abner agrees, "Let them arise." Kyle McCarter is certainly correct in agreeing with Eissfeldt (1951:118-27; 1952:55-59) and de Vaux (1966) that "lighthearted competition" is not what is implied by this language of sport. Rather, the contest is "a completely serious fight," (McCarter, 1984:95) and it ends in the death of both groups of twelve men, the outcome thus not being a victory for one side or the other. Nevertheless the use of the verb "to play" implies a particular way of looking at war that equates war with games (de Vaux, 1966:130; Vermeule:85), again one quite different from the view of war found in the ban as sacrifice, the ban as God's justice, or the priestly war traditions. The stylized form of engagement described for these single encounters in which each man grasps his opponent by the head in a wrestling style of combat points to the border where the warrior's games meet war.

If the ban as sacrifice suggests that victory sometimes requires that God receive his due in enemy killed—hence the killing—and the ban as God's justice that the enemy deserves to die and be rooted out like an infectious fungus—hence the killing—the image of battle as contest or game approaches the killing as a deadly matter of skill, training, luck, and of course divine approval. The killing has to do with ego, quest for glory, is more individualized, and also more limited. It is the work of professionals and excludes the killing of non-combatants altogether. In fact, one might suggest the warriors adhere to a code (Aho:169–173).

Codes, Combat, and Kin

The scene at 2 Sam 2:12–16 continues with the wider confrontation at v. 17, a fierce battle between the men of David and the men of Saul, and the Davidic forces gain the upper hand. Asahel, the brother of David's general Joab, follows Abner the opposing general. The latter calls to him "Turn aside from following me. What purpose would it serve for me to strike you to the ground? How could I face your brother Joab?" (2:22). Abner is portrayed as having feelings of loyalty or obligation towards Joab though the former is related by family to Saul, a Benjaminite, and the latter to David, a Judahite. An implicit soldierly camaraderie and respect between peers trained for the same career and a sense of fair play are seen in this portrayal. The lad Asahel is no match for the more experienced Abner. Again a certain noble gamesmanship is found. But the impetuous youth will not abandon his pursuit and Abner kills him. Like de Vaux (1966:128–29) one is moved to comparisons with the classical Greek epic tradition, for the description of Asahel's death at 2 Sam 2:23 is reminiscent of many scenes in the *Iliad* (e.g., in Book 13:410–12, 545–47, 567–73, 615–18). "And Abner struck him through the belly with the butt of his spear, and the spear came out through his back" (2 Sam 2:23).

The issue of kinship is important in this biblical war tradition, though "kinship" is understood narrowly or broadly, depending on the passage. Joab never forgets Abner's slaying of his brother and bides his time, finally taking vengeance (2 Sam 3:26–27). The need to avenge his brother's death overrides other loyalties to David and to the unified state that David is able to establish in Israel.

By the same token, 2 Sam 2:24–28, the description of the continuing battle in which the confrontation between Asahel and Abner is a close-up scene, shows Abner and Joab communicating and negotiating to call a temporary truce because the fighters are all "kinsmen," literally "brothers."

> Abner called to Joab and said "Must the sword devour forever? Don't you know that it will be bitter in the end? How long will you refrain from telling the people to turn back from pursuing their kin?" (2 Sam 2:26).

Joab responds sympathetically to his counterpart and halts the fighting, again referring to the enemy troops as "kin" or "brothers" (2 Sam 2:27). "Kin" is understood by the biblical writer to be an all-Israelite designation. As discussed in the Introduction the code of fair play—respect for truce, attempts to limit the destruction evidenced by 2 Sam 2:12–32—is upheld within the group, however "inside-the-group" is defined. In the war texts of the Hebrew Scriptures, that group is usually not defined family by family, village by village, lineage by lineage, or tribe by tribe but by the notion of Israel as a whole. To create such an image of unity—the fiction perpetuated and created especially by the genealogies—is in fact one of the interests and concerns of the writers in biblical tradition. It is indeed central to the belief system revealed by the Hebrew Scriptures that Israel is one people of shared lineage and identity. The biblical tales both reflect and help to shape this identity. The people may be described as wracked by civil war or divided about what constitutes heresy and orthodoxy, but for the most part an image of Israel as a unified group overshadows hints of what must have been the actual sociological realities that scholars such as de Geus and Lemche have worked so hard to uncover. The image of Israel as kin certainly dominates the war texts. It is as strong in its own way in this chivalric literature of war as in the texts about the ban as God's justice in which Israel is clearly demarcated from foreigners deserving extermination. Indeed, one might say that the concern with Israel as kin is more marked in the bardic texts of war than in those concerning the ban as God's justice, for in the latter disloyal Israelites become the unclean "Other" who also must be exterminated whereas in texts such as 2 Sam 2:26, a certain code applies among kin that discourages such total killing. That is, Saul and David's troops and generals might have been portrayed as considering the "Other" worthy of banning but this is not the case. The warrior's code of the bardic tradition begins to look more like a secular, western just-war doctrine, to be contrasted with the religious crusade. (For a fascinating parallel in western Christian tradition see the trajectory from chivalric to just-war codes drawn by Johnson, 1975:25.)

Limitations in Non-Bardic Texts: Kin and Non-Kin

A passage of similar ideology concerning the sparing of kin is 1 Kgs 12:21–24 (2 Chron 11:1–4). This passage is set at the time of the schism between the North (Israel) and the South (Judah). David united these two regions and the whole was maintained by Solomon, but at the accession of his son Rehoboam, the North breaks away from the South under a leader named Jeroboam.

Some traditions preserved in the Deuteronomic History are so strongly attached to the Davidic dynasty that disloyalty to it could be regarded as motivation for invoking the ban. Indeed, in 1 Kgs 12:25–13:34 Jeroboam is described as a doomed, idolatrous apostate. But 1 Kgs 12:21–24 breathes of a different spirit. Rehoboam masses his troops to win back the North (1 Kgs 12:21), but an oracle comes from God through the prophet Shemaiah: "Thus says the Lord, 'You shall not go up, you shall not fight with your kin, the people of Israel. Let each man return to his house, for from me is this pronouncement'" (1 Kgs 12:24). God is thus put on the side of holding peace among Israelites.

The same spirit is found in 2 Chronicles (28:5–15), a work that as a whole genuinely eschews some of the more brutal aspects of other biblical ideologies of war. (For a brief but ethically conscious treatment of this passage, see Luria:256–59.) Israel, which remains a separate kingdom after the schism discussed above, had united with Aram against Judah and successfully defeated them. Israel is described as taking captive 200,000 "of their kin, women, sons, and daughters; they also despoiled them of much booty, and brought the booty to Samaria (the capital of Israel)" (28:8).

> And there, was a prophet of God, Oded was his name. He went before the army that had come to Samaria and said to them "Behold, because the Lord, God of your ancestors was angry with Judah, he gave them into your hands, but you have killed them with a rage that reaches to the sky. And now, you say you are going to subjugate the people of Judah and Jerusalem as male and female slaves for yourselves, but is it not precisely among yourselves that are (found) wrong-doings against the Lord your God? Rather, listen to me and return the prisoners you have captured from your kin, for the anger of God is upon you" (2 Chron 28:9–11).

Oded makes clear that Judah has been defeated because God willed it so as a punishment, but Israel is nevertheless required to treat these prisoners with generosity and forgiveness lest they add to their own sins the sin of enslaving and maltreating their own people. The phrase "with a rage that reaches to the sky" very clearly implies that they fought with excess and speaks in favor of limits when fighting kin (see also Am 1:11).

The warnings of Oded are heeded. The warriors hand over their prisoners to community leaders (28:14), and the prisoners are given support. Those who are naked are clothed; they are given sandals, food, and water. Those too weak to walk are led on donkeys and the captives and all the booty are brought to Jericho in Judah (28:14–15).

A fascinating parallel to this text that extends the theme of generous treatment of prisoners of war to non-Israelites, non-kin, is found at 2 Kgs 6:22–23. Here too is the theme that the victory is of God; humans do not necessarily have the right to profit from the victory that comes not from them. In this respect 2 Kgs 6:22–23 admits of some conceptual connections to the ban texts, especially the ban as sacrifice in which the best spoil is not man's but God's, but the resulting ideology of war is radically different, the policy toward human life to preserve it. The context of 2 Kgs 6:22–23 is a miraculous escape from Aramaean invaders. The Israelites are saved when God blinds the attacking forces as requested by Elisha the prophet. (On the nature of the blindness see La Barbera:642–44.) The role of the prophet's efficacious prayer and the miracle account in which Israel is saved in war without raising their own hands is a popular biblical pattern, found in the Exodus account and especially in late biblical material. It is in fact the link to an ideology that has more in common with non-violence than with just-war ideologies, a view of war discussed in chapter 7. In this context, our interest is in Elisha's insistence that the Aramaean prisoners be treated as guests and returned home. He declares (vv. 22–23)

> Set food and water before them so that they might eat and drink and let them go to their master. And they feted them with a great feast; after they ate and drank, he sent them off and they went to their master. And the Aramaean forces did not again come against the land of Israel.

The clear message is that proper treatment of the enemy—combined of course with temporary blindness—might stun him into respect. In terms of the style and content, 2 Chron 28:5–15 and 2 Kgs 6:22–23 are not the sort of bardic-style literature discussed above but share with these texts an interesting aspect of war ideology that has to do with limits on killing and respect for prisoners. 2 Kgs 6:22–23 extends the respect beyond kin.

Reciprocity of Various Sorts

The loyalty shown to kin and an implicit code of fair play in war is shown extending to non-Israelite enemies also at Judges 8:18–21. The tale of Gideon is rich in the bardic literary qualities found in such abundance in the stories of David. At Judg 8:18–21, Gideon interrogates Zebaḥ and Zalmuna, kings of Midian, whom he has captured in battle. He asks the kings "Where are the men you killed in Tabor" and they respond "They looked just like you, each one resembling king's sons." Gideon responds that these men were his brothers, "the sons of my mother," and vows in God's name, "As the Lord lives, had you allowed them to live I would not have killed you" (8:19).

No sacrificial ban is involved or a question of killing these Midianites as idolaters. Rather the issue is one of reciprocity and fairness in war intertwined with issues of loyalty to one's kin—here immediate, literal family kin is meant and not a wider Israelite kinship. The Midianite kings know they must die; implicitly they share a code with Gideon, the enemy warrior chief.

Gideon instructs his eldest son to kill them, but the young man, a less experienced soldier than his father, hesitates. "He was afraid for he was still a youth." (8:20) This statement acknowledges the power of kingship and the respect due kings, but even more important acknowledges that it is not easy to kill, even in a war setting, even when a code allows for just vengeance. The kings themselves speak to Gideon: "You yourself get up and fall upon us for the measure of the man is his might (or as the man is, so is his valor)." Gideon is "a man" and kills them with dispatch. This interchange and the earlier one reveal a remarkable degree of respect between warriors, acceptance of one's fate in war, and like the encounter between Asahel and Abner the theme that a man should face his equal in combat.

An important issue in battle encounters, discussed above in terms of a code of fair play, has to do with division and distribution of spoil. We took special note of 2 Chron 28:9–11 in which stripping the enemy of booty when the enemy is one's own kin is deemed improper.

Dividing the Spoil

Many of the bardic-style texts have to do with fair distribution of spoil and, in fact, with arguments concerning the booty. In contrast, again, to both banning traditions and the priestly tradition of Numbers 31, acquisition of the enemy's wealth and enhancement of one's own prestige and power are some of the objects of the fighting. These men are seekers of glory as are their Achaian counterparts whose quarrels over spoil provide the background of the *Iliad*.

In Judg 8:1-3, Gideon who is said to be of the clan of Abiezer (Judg 6:11), is described as being upbraided by the Ephraimites for not having invited them to participate in the battle against Zebaḥ and Zalmunna and thus to enjoy the spoil from that battle. Jephthah, another chieftain, faces a similar charge from Ephraimites at Judg 12:1-3 and the two forces end up coming to blows.

The motif of the feud over spoil is a traditional one from a literary perspective. From a political perspective, control over distribution of the spoil or consolidation of the power to take the spoil indicates that an author is creating or describing a more centralized form of political structure than, for example, is imagined in Judges. Thus at 1 Sam 30:21-31 the would-be king of all Israel, David, is described as making fair and all-inclusive rules for distribution of spoil among warriors, allocating some of the wealth for those who might be helpful in supporting his kingship.

The plot of the larger story concluded by the distribution of spoil is also worth mentioning within this chapter on the bardic literature of war, for again it has to do with the search for glory, the bonds between kin, just causes for fighting, a code among warriors—in this case for the distribution of spoil—and an expectation that you will do to the enemy what they do to you. The story of 1 Samuel 30 is a Robin Hood-like tale of the hero. Amalekites raid the Negeb and Ziklag. This term "to raid" or "to ambush" is found frequently in the warring texts we are exploring under the heading of bardic literature (Judg 9:33, 44; 1 Sam 23:27; 1 Sam 27:10) and creates an impression of banditry, adventure, and small war parties making quick incursions into enemy camps.

In their raid, the Amalekites have burned Ziklag, David's holding as vassal of Achish, and taken goods and people among whom are David's wives and children. David consults the oracle to see if conditions are favorable for counter-attack (1 Sam 30:8). This is a regular and frequently found feature of undertaking war in various biblical texts (e.g. 1 Sam 23:4-5; 2 Sam 5:17-25 = 1 Chron 14:8-17). David is aided in his victory by an Egyptian, a servant of an Amalekite. The man is found languishing along the way "in the open country" (Sam 30:11). Before even knowing his identity

David and his men give him food and drink and revive him. It turns out that the Amalekites had left him behind without food or water because he had fallen ill. They had indeed not extended a code of loyalty or care to one of their own party. Amalekites never receive favorable reviews by biblical authors, no matter in which war trajectory they are found. The man helps David to find the enemy camp in return for a promise that David will protect him. Then follows the victory as promised by God. All women and booty are returned unharmed along with the enemies' spoil, which is then fairly distributed to all of David's men, including those who did not participate in the battle. In this way conquered spoil unifies rather than divides the people.

An interesting parallel to this typical adventure of the hero is found in Genesis 14. Abram's nephew Lot, his women, retainers, and goods are taken by Chedorlaomer of Elam and his allies when he attacks the kings of Sodom and Gomorrah. Like David, Abram is informed of the incursion in this case by one who had escaped, and pursues the enemy, successfully defeating them and rescuing his relatives and their household. This battle of Abram, so like 1 Samuel 30, and so unlike the patriarchal material surrounding it, also ends on matters of spoil and distribution. In this case following a presentation of bread and wine and of thanks to God by Abram's ally one King Melchizedek of Salem, "a priest of God Most High," Abram gives Melchizedek one tenth of "everything" (Gen 14:20). The "everything" probably refers to booty taken; in v. 16 Abram is described as taking all the "goods" or "property," a term referring to moveable possessions of all kinds. Further, he refuses Sodom's generous offer to keep the remaining goods while Sodom would take the people (14:21). (On problems in interpreting who receives what see Emerton, 1971b:405-6.) Abram will take only enough to cover what his soldiers have eaten and the share of the chief warriors who had gone with him, lest the king of Sodom be able to say that he had made Abram rich (Gen 14:22-24).

Mock-Heroic

Both 1 Samuel 30 and Genesis 14 present just cause for war, the abduction of kin. Both contain heroic victories, very briefly described, and a warrior hero who shows proper respect to his God, the origin of all victory. Both, moreover, are concerned with the disposition of spoil. Both men are portrayed as fair and generous. There are some interesting differences, however. Whereas David's dividing of spoil is seen in clear political—in fact politically unifying—terms that have to do with the transition from bandit chief to head of a larger group (contrast the squabbles in Judg 8:1–3 and 12:1–3), Abram gives spoil to a king-priest not mentioned previously in the tale and then denies spoil to himself. On some levels, both tales suit the sort of bardic or heroic ideology of war we have been discussing. Both show the concern with justness and code as well as the interests in heroic adventure found in this trajectory. Whereas the author of 1 Samuel 30 paints a hero ready to become king through dealing and diplomacy, the author of Genesis 14 creates a more independent hero, a loner who fights only to protect kin and not to obtain spoil. It is an ennobling portrait of Abram (Emerton, 1971b:432) contrasting with the trickster of Genesis 12 and the bargainer of Genesis 18. The latter are popular portraits, the former more the purview of chivalry, though we agree with Westermann and others that Genesis 14 is probably a late, post-monarchic—we would say "mock-heroic"—piece (Westermann, 1985, Vol. 2:192–93). A true bardic hero would revel in his spoil and his glory.

Conclusions

The war portrayals examined in this chapter reveal a code of fair play, limitation, and reciprocity in which warriors from opposing sides regard one another with respect, in which the bond between kin-at-war remains pronounced, and in which a man seeks to fight his equal in skill, valor, and experience. The victories glorify the noble heroes involved in them, and the taking of spoil is part of the reward. War itself is equated with sport, a manly exercise. The chivalric texts of the Hebrew Bible impose a patina of noble order on the chaos that is real war. Aspects of this chivalric code appear also in other texts such as 2 Chronicles 28 and 2 Kgs 6:22–23, enjoining care for prisoners—in the latter case non-kin. We have seen in the bardic texts the outlines of a just war code especially pertaining to *jus in bello*, a code of conduct shared by fighters on the same side and by enemies. The fight is for glory and booty as well as for the soldiers' belief in their cause, and so distribution of spoil is an issue in this sort of literature. Genesis 14 extends the fairness in booty-taking to the point that the hero denies himself spoil altogether. In this way, the hero of the tale, Abram, is made to look completely noble, unmercenary, and selfless in a fairly atypical sort of bardic portrayal that supports the description of Genesis 14 as "mock-heroic."

Kin is defined in this bardic literature, for the most part, in all-Israelite terms that support an image of unity and nationalism, though the tale of death and vengeance involving Asahel, Abner, and Joab is a family feud and Gideon expresses special loyalty to his own brothers, killing the enemy, as does Joab, in apparent vengeance over the death of his kin. In the disagreements over spoil, bardic authors imagine the way in which a breakdown in the unity of the group might occur.

The recurring images and language of these texts, and the larger recurring patterns of content betoken traditional-style literature in which there is a way to describe such war portrayals. Of course this is true of most slices of biblical narration—the ban texts too reuse language and imagery and are stunningly shocking in the monotony of their recurring refrains about the taking of life.

The dialogue in the "bardic" war portrayals is distinguishes its particular traditional style. Instead of the tautness and terseness that characterize some of the dialogue in the Hebrew Scriptures, these texts are fuller, richer, artfully realistic in emotional content and effect. Goliath taunts David at some length using proverbial language equating insult with being treated like a dog. The Midianite kings Zebah and Zalmuna virtually wax eloquent in describing to Gideon his brothers whom they have killed. Like Goliath they speak in a proverb, in this case to challenge the hero to kill them or perhaps even to welcome their death at the hands of a hero worthy of them (Judg 8:18–21).

Descriptions are also more detailed than usual in Hebrew Scripture. Goliath's armament is described in great detail: the helmet (1 Sam 17:5); the coat of mail (1 Sam 17:5); the greaves, his javelin, his spear (1 Sam 17:6–7). The death of Asahel is described anatomically (2 Sam 2:23). Virtual catalogues are provided of the men of valor and their deeds at 2 Sam 21:15–22 and 23:8–39, reminiscent of similar collections of material in the *Iliad* (e.g. 1:494–759; 1:763–877). The catalogue of kings at the beginning of Genesis 14 imitates this bardic style.

Taken as a group, these war texts reveal a courtly, even a chivalric view of war that has more in common with a work such as the *Iliad* than with the banning texts explored in chapters 1 and 2. The question arises whether these texts reflect war values held by courtier fighters in the early period of the monarchy and just before the establishment of the monarchy or whether they are examples of a stylized international epic form that reports warring activities in certain ways. Do these war portrayals, like European medieval chivalric romances, reflect something quite different from the way real human beings interacted in actual life settings? The least one can say is that these war portrayals reflect an idealization of combat, its victors, and its motivations. In this way, war is glorified and made palatable, a game of sorts, a fair game, for the best man wins. Who would want to preserve such an ideology? Whom does it benefit? It certainly makes for good narration—the entertainment factor is an important one. Like old movies starring John Wayne, such stories endow war with alluring excitement and macho respectability, evoking the competitive side of people in which violent combat is equated with sport. The bardic literature of war thus helps to perpetuate warring behavior, perhaps to encourage it, as much as the ban portrayals discussed in chapter 2. Is it then the literature of court bards produced for the pleasure and indoctrination of courtiers that becomes everyone's national epic, told in town squares? Is it a men's literature originally written for men in an androcentric culture?

Limitations on the knowledge of Israelite social history preclude drawing definite conclusions. The unknown includes the training by which bards learned narrative traditions, the contexts in which they produced and performed them, and the way in which these traditions became a part of the corpus that scholars call the Deuteronomic History. My own guess would be that these materials stem from a courtly bardic tradition produced in glorification of a young nation state, its king, its "mighty men," and the heroes of previous generations.

5

The Ideology of Tricksterism

Some traditional narratives in the Hebrew Scriptures project a war ideology quite different from that of the bardic literature discussed in chapter 4. These are tales of victory via trickery found in Genesis 34, the confrontation with the Shechemites over the rape of Dinah; in Judges 14–15, Samson's confrontations with the Philistines; in Judges 3:15–30, Ehud's guerilla-style assassination of Eglon that initiates a larger battle with the Moabites; and in Judges 4:17–24 and 5:24–31, Jael's assassination of the Canaanite general Sisera, the conclusion of an Israelite victory in which "no one (of the enemy) was left" (Judges 4:16).

This group of war portrayals has many features in common with the bardic traditions: several of the scenes are cameos set within larger wars; their style is "economically" repetitive, the same language being used to convey the same piece of content within the tale; their essential plots or patterns of content are found elsewhere in the Hebrew Scriptures and in a wider range of non-biblical folk narrative traditions. However, whereas the pattern of warring in the bardic tales involves direct confrontation between enemies, frequently the trading of taunts, and a shared code of honor, confrontation in the trickster tales relies upon deception, an ethic entirely at odds with a soldier's code of honor. The hero or heroine achieves victory by deceiving the enemy. The warring, moreover, in at least three of these scenes is related to matters of human sexuality: in two cases, clumsy attempts to establish marital relations between enemy

106

groups; in the other, a metaphorical equation between eroticism and death. The sexual is equated with the political; the one serves as a comment on the other, as in so many tales of those who employ trickery to alter their marginal status (Niditch, 1987:54; 1989; 1990:616–17).

The Rape of Dinah: Genesis 34

This tale begins with a rape. As in the Greek Trojan War tradition or the biblical tale of Judges 19–21, the cause for war involves the misuse by men of a woman belonging to another man or men. From a feminist perspective, one of the most marked features of such tales of woman-stealing is the minor role played by the women in the stories about their victimization. The stories are not primarily about the men's relations to the women who have suffered violence, but about the relations between the men of the opposing groups (Rubin). This is true too of tales of proper marriage. Rachel and Leah, for example, link Laban and Jacob in alternating acts of cooperation and angry contest. In this case as in Judges 19–21 and the Trojan theme, the woman is a catalyst for war. Instead of being an acceptable item of exchange joining groups of men, she becomes a just cause for vengeance and the severing of ties.

The motif of stealing or raping the women of another group is a very ancient one in traditional narrative, and speaks to one of the most basic dilemmas in human social relations—namely how to steer the proper course between endogamy and exogamy. This issue ultimately has to do with relations between those perceived as "us" versus those perceived as "them" and reduces to the basics of human interaction essential questions of war and peace. Marriage to someone belonging to a distant or alien group is just as danger-ous as incestuous marriage to a member of one's own group who is too close a relative. Just as proper marital relations are constructive and peace-making, relations formed by rape, incest, or wife-stealing are destructive. To know how a group defines whom it is proper to marry and how it is proper to marry is to know a great deal about their sense of self and the other. The tale of Dinah cannot be read as a comment on specific marriage customs the breach of which are causes for war in ancient Israel, for its pattern of content, linking rape and war, is universal. But the way these familiar and universal motifs are treated in Genesis 34 allows for comment on the implicit attitude to "the Other" found in the tale, its definition of "the group," its view of women, and its ideology of war, an ideology expressed in the narrative pattern of the trickster.

The Story

Dinah who has gone to visit some of the non-Israelite neighbor women (literally "the daughters of the land") is raped by Shechem, Son of Hamor the Hittite, prince of the area. The Hebrew reads he took her, lay (with) her, and raped her. The "rape" term literally means to afflict or oppress—thus are the Israelites treated by Pharaoh in Egypt. In spite of the etymology of rape, the biblical narrator does not treat Shechem's rape as an act of violence and considers it compatible with love. At least so Shechem's attitude is portrayed. The language of v. 3 thus softens: "His (Shechem's) soul clung to Dinah . . . he loved the girl and spoke coaxingly to her (literally 'upon her heart')," and asked his father to obtain her for his wife. The language of victimization resumes in Gen 34:5. Jacob heard that he (Shechem) had sullied his daughter, literally "rendered her unclean." The body, especially the woman's body, is a vessel that can be rendered unclean, a commodity, like an edible, that can be made unfit for consumption by improper use or storage.

Jacob, the father, is silent about the matter, but Dinah's brothers are enraged. The narrative paints a real difference between the more patient, acquiescent, deal-making old men and the impatient youths who grab what they want (in the case of Shechem) or are quick to vengeance (in the case of Dinah's brothers). Also present is an interesting tradition of brothers who are their sisters' protectors and fathers who are impotent and unprotecting. Thus, later in the Book of 2 Samuel, Absalom avenges the rape of his sister Tamar by their half-brother Amnon, while King David, their father, holds his peace (2 Sam 13:21-29). Shechem, they say, has committed an outrage in Israel. The term used for outrage is the same as that used for the crime of the Gibeonites who rape the Levite's woman in

Judges 19 (see also Josh 7:15). The sons of Jacob—and the point of view they represent—accuse Shechem of acting in a barbarous fashion, breaking accepted rules of civilized interaction (34:7). Throughout Dinah is called "daughter of Jacob," for the injury is done to Jacob and his sons and not only to Dinah. Dinah herself recedes into the background and is mentioned only once more at the end of the tale, for though she is central to the story—without her there would be no plot—the story is not about her, but about the contest for honor and the struggle for power between two groups of men linked by her.

Shechem's father comes to Jacob and his sons offering a deal. If they will give Dinah to his son, then regular in-marrying relations can be established between the two groups, exchanges of women in marriage and rights to dwell in the land and ply trade for the sons of Jacob. Shechem offers a generous bride-price, as much as Jacob wishes, in order to win the girl in an acceptable way that would, in effect, set aright his improperly having helped himself to Dinah's sexuality without the sanction of the men around her.

The sons of Jacob respond in deception (34:14): "We cannot do this thing to give our sister to a man who is not circumcised; it is a disgrace among us." If the men on Shechem's side will agree to become circumcised like them, then the sons of Jacob and the sons of Hamor will become one people and Dinah will become the wife of Shechem. Hamor and his son agree to the terms (34:18) as do their fellow citizens. All the men are circumcised, and while they are indisposed by the surgery, Simeon and Levi, the full-brothers of Dinah, swoop down on the unsuspecting Shechemites with their swords, killing every male. They take Dinah back with them along with their enemy's booty, sheep, cattle, and donkeys, their wealth, whatever was the town, field, and households, including their children and their wives. In this way, they employ trickery involving the seat of male reproductive power to despoil those who had despoiled their sister. The tale's irony is grounded in themes of sexuality and vengeance. Sexual control, moreover, is a political matter. The brothers have restored the honor of Jacob's household and repossessed the woman, thereby rejecting Shechemite overtures that would eliminate the difference between Israelite and Other, a contrast essential to the author's self-definition.

The Ideology: Genesis 34 in a Spectrum

In one of the ranges of war portrayals discussed in the Introduction, Genesis 34 probably belongs under the heading feud within a pre-state society. The issue is woman-stealing and male honor; the matter is between small groups tracing lineages to a single head of household; the fighting is done by the groups' males and not by professionals; no governmental authority is assumed. This portrayal does not mean that Genesis 34 is an early, pre-monarchic text nor its war ideology early. The narrative does, however, tell us a great deal about its author's ideology of war and larger world-view. Israel is pictured as a spunky but insecure pastoral people set apart from the uncircumcised city folk. Sentiments of us versus them are as strong as in the ban as God's justice and the priestly tradition of Numbers 31. Israel is a whole apart from the peoples of the land. The woman is an item of exchange who can be damaged and rendered unclean through wrong sorts of sexual contact, but adult foreign women are not necessarily regarded as infected and untouchable simply by being of the other group. Victory is not achieved by noble warriors as in the bardic tradition nor by crusaders aided by God in God's cause of vengeance as in the ban as God's justice or priestly trajectories, nor is the enemy's death an offering to a sacrifice-hungry deity. Victory is via trickery. No code of equality and honesty between combatants is found, for the battle is not between equals, warriors all.

Deception is one of the ways marginal people imagine themselves improving their situation at the expense of those with greater power, as in the many underdog tales of Genesis or the Afro-American tradition of trickster-tales (Niditch, 1987:44–50). The sons of Jacob use their own wits to succeed. God's help is not mentioned. And yet, their success is of an unstable variety as are all tricksters' victories. Abram deceives Pharaoh only to be thrown out of town (Genesis 12), Jacob deceives Esau and suffers exile and the prospect of again confronting his brother, and so on. The old trickster himself, Jacob, warns his hot-headed sons at Gen 34:30: "You have brought trouble upon me by making me hated among the inhabitants of the land . . . they will gather against me, strike me, and I shall be destroyed, myself and my household."

The sons have the last word, again an appeal to honor based upon the man's capacity to protect his women. "Should he be allowed to treat our sister like a harlot?!" The victory, however, is not neat or final as the ḥērem texts would have it. This tale of war comes from a time and people who enjoy and find relevant the image of Israelites as tricksters who defy those who would control them or theirs. They do not defy the enemy directly, but employ wit, wile, and deception and assume that no victories are final or neat. Theirs is a world-view that differs strongly from the more aristocratic establishment-generated idealism of the bardic texts (In this context, see Gen 49:5–7).

Samson and the Timnites

The beautifully crafted cycle of stories telling the life and adventures of the super-hero Samson shares with Genesis 34 motifs of the wrong sort of marital overtures between Israelite and non-Israelite, confrontation through deception, and the overt violence between men that breaks out because of the desire to control the woman of one group. The constellation of women, sexuality, tricksterism, and combat recurs several times in the narrative of Samson (Judges 13–16). The tale that has the most in common with Genesis 34 in world-view and implicit war ideology is Samson's attempt to acquire a wife from among the Philistines and the outcome of that foray in Judges 14–15.

Samson sees a Philistine woman in Timnah and wants her (14:1). His mother and father try to discourage him, their words clearly setting up the theme of Israelite versus non-Israelite that is so strong in the Samson cycle as a whole. "Is there not a woman among your kin or in all (our) people that you have to go take a woman from the uncircumcised Philistines?" (Judg 14:3). They, like Dinah's brothers, consider such a union a "disgrace." Samson persists—the biblical narrator tells us that Samson must persist because God "seeks an opportunity (to act) against the Philistines. At that time the Philistines ruled over Israel." (14:4)

On his way to meet the woman of Timnah, Samson kills a lion with bare hands. When he returns to marry her he notices that a swarm of honey bees has established its home in the lion's carcass. At the marriage feast, a riddling contest takes place. If the Timnites can solve Samson's riddle he will give them thirty linen garments and thirty festal garments. If he wins the contest, they must give the gift to him. The riddling contest, like the mock combat, is a part of wedding rituals throughout the world. Like the taunting among warriors discussed above, ideally, these sorts of confrontation allow groups or individuals who distrust one another as the "Other" to act out their animosities in a safe way so that no one is actually hurt (Noy; Slotkin:153–55).

Samson's riddle, however, involves trickery:

> From the eater comes something to eat
> and from the strong comes something sweet.
> (trans. Camp and Fontaine:138)

Whereas his riddle could be answered in sexual terms (Nel:534–45; Crenshaw 1978:99–120; Camp and Fontaine:141–42), his experience with the lion provides a second more literal response, known only to himself. The Timnites can discover the answer about the honey and the lion only by forcing the young bride to be their informant. The riddling contest is a vying for status. The men's status here as in Genesis 34 is contingent upon who controls the woman. Hence, Samson's sexually charged proverbial response to the Philistines,

> If you had not plowed with my heifer,
> you would not have found out my riddle.
> (trans. Camp and Fontaine:147)

In a rage, Samson obtains his payment of the bet by killing thirty Ashkelonites, and then returns to his father's house.

The girl's father responds by giving her to another man. When Samson comes looking for her and finds out she has been given to another, he sends foxes with torches attached to their tales to burn the Philistines' standing grain, vineyards, and olive groves. He is himself, after all, a man of the beasts. The Philistines respond by killing the young woman and her father. Like Dinah, she is the silent catalyst of all that goes on around her and yet the story is about honor and relations between two groups of men. In response to the death of his wife, Samson wreaks havoc among the Philistines, slaughtering them "hip and thigh" (15:8). The tale of violence continues and escalates.

Motifs of sex, violence, and trickery spin the contest for power between the one who is outside the group and those with the power. Samson, alone with his Philistine hosts, is the lone outsider attempting to put himself on an equal footing with them as he acquires one of their women as wife. So the Israelites as a whole are portrayed in Judges as the marginal people, harassed by better armed, wealthier Canaanite and Philistine competitors in the land. The narrator sets the scene at 14:4 and the Judahites themselves remind Samson, "Do you not know that the Philistines rule over us?" (15:11). They like Jacob in Genesis fear those with power over them. While Samson's combat is portrayed in bigger-than-life epic terms involving one man against Philistine hordes, nevertheless it contains implicit political and war ideologies steeped in indirection and deception, the weapons of the marginal. Samson uses his own massive power as a secret weapon at 15:14 and 16:3 and again when the Philistines seek to entrap him at Delilah's (Judg 16:4–14). Only when he abandons deception and reveals the truth about his strength is he overpowered. The distrust of the enemy is equalled by an implicit insecurity in one's own power. No implicit guilt complicates the killing in contrast to both banning traditions and the priestly ideology of Numbers 31, nor is the killing ever directed inside the group. No respect is found for the enemy in contrast to the bardic code. The trickster ideology of war has the potential to produce unabashedly and uncontrolledly violent behavior, a war ideology of the oppressed that is a step away from guerilla warfare and terrorism.

Jael: Sexuality, Tricksterism, and Violence

The story of Jael's assassination of the Canaanite general Sisera is found in prose and poetic accounts in Judges 4 and 5. Each version creates a tense atmosphere of alluring sexuality and deception that leads to a visceral but coolly described act of violence. Jael is portrayed as a seducer-destroyer who sets the man at his ease with offers of comfort and security and then kills him. Disguising herself as his savior, Jael beckons the fleeing Sisera to her tent. The

Israelites have routed the forces of their Canaanite enemies and the general needs a hideout. Mother-like and siren-like she says, "Turn to me, don't be afraid" (Judg 4:18). Trustingly, he turns aside and enters her tent where she covers him with a rug. The opening images are of trust, warmth, and protection (Alter, 1985:48–49). He asks for a bit of water but she brings him milk and "gives him a drink"— a single verb literally meaning causes him to drink—and the prose account repeats "she covers him." Images of mother with child come to mind. Mother becomes lover becomes exterminator in Judg 4:21 as Jael comes to Sisera in secret (See Alter, 1985:48–49). The "come" verb is often used in the Hebrew Scriptures to indicate sexual entry. The word meaning "in secret" creates a mood of mystery and eroticism. So Ruth comes to Boaz "in secret" at the threshing floor (Ruth 3:7). But Jael comes not for love but to pierce the temple of Sisera's head with a tent peg. Robert Alter has called attention to the phallic quality of Jael's killing of Sisera at 4:21 (1985:43–49). Motifs of eroticism and death, feminine seduction, and machismo strength are even more exquisitely intertwined in the poetic account in 5:27 in which it is made clear that through a deception, grounded in her qualities as woman, Jael has turned her more powerful male enemy into a woman, despoiled by her.

> Between her legs he knelt, he fell, he lay
> Between her legs he knelt, he fell
> Where he knelt, there he fell despoiled.

The language has a rhythmic, intoning, repetitive quality, capturing Sisera's death throes upon his knees, falling lower, lying, dying (see Alter, 1985:45). Each image, however, equates the act of dying with the act of sex (Zakovitch; Niditch, 1989; Alter, 1985:43–49). The legs, like the feet and hands, are a euphemism in biblical Hebrew for the genitals. Thus the afterbirth emerges from between a woman's legs (Deut 28:57; see also Ezek 16:25; Isa 7:20; Judg 3:24; 1 Sam 24:3). The term kneeling is used in a context of defeat and death, paired as here with the verb "to fall" at Ps 20:8 (v. 9 in Hebrew), but "to kneel" is also found in an overtly sexual context at Job 31:10 paired with another sexual euphemism "to grind" (cf. Isa 47:2; Pope:231).

If my heart has been enticed by a woman,
And at my neighbor's door I have lain in wait,
Let my wife "grind" for another,
Upon her may others kneel.
(Job 31:9-10)

Job, despairing in his illness and maintaining his innocence, declares in an oath that another may violate his wife if he himself has committed a sexual sin. The verb "to lie" is also frequently associated with death and defeat. To die is "to lie or sleep with one's ancestors" (1 Kgs 1:21; 2 Kgs 14:22). Battle images of death employing the verb "to lie" are found at Ezek 32:29; 32:21. "To lie," however, is frequently also used in Hebrew Scriptures in a sexual context [Gen 19:32, 34, 35; 34:2, 7 (the rape of Dinah discussed above); Gen 35:22; 1 Sam 2:22; Gen 39:10, 12, 14; Lev 20:11, 12, 13, 20, etc.]. Finally the word "despoiled" or "dealt violently with" is associated with the destruction of enemies (Isa 15:1; 23:1; Jer 47:4) but is used in an erotic metpahor at Jer 4:30 as Jeremiah compares an unfaithful Israel to a sleazy harlot, beautifying herself for her lovers.

And you are despoiled.
What are you doing in dressing in scarlet
in decking yourself with golden ornaments
in widening your eyes with make-up . . .

In this way, the poet of Judges 5 creates imagery rich in eroticism and death. In contrast to the tale of Dinah, it is the woman who despoils the man, he who dies ruined and helpless in the position of a would-be supplicant or lover. Alter has suggested that this image of Sisera's death may be "an ironic glance at the time-honored martial custom of rape" (Alter, 1985:49–84) and like others (Levine:83–84) has pointed to the ironic juxtaposition in the poem of Sisera's death described in 5:27 and the hopes of his mother and her ladies-in-waiting who await his return from battle.

"Out of the window she peered,
   the mother of Sisera gazed through the lattice
'Why is his chariot so long in coming?
   Why tarry the hoofbeats of his chariots?'
Her wisest ladies make answer
   indeed, she answers the question herself:

'Are they not finding and dividing the spoil?—
A girl or two for every man . . .'"
(trans. NRSV Judg 5:28–30)

His mother, portrayed as an aristocratic woman living in a home with lattice-work windows, surrounded by a cortege, waits for the noble warrior who has gone to battle in a horse-drawn chariot. He will not return, having been entrapped by a woman in a tent who supports the Israelite cause. Instead of the genuine love and loyalty expressed by his mother and her ladies he has found deception and death. Instead of obtaining woman booty (literally called by the root for "womb" at Judges 5:30) he has been womanized.

The image of the defeated warrior as a subdued or raped woman in classical Greek material has been explored by Emily Vermeule.

> In a duel, an isolated world inside the main battle, one soldier must be the female partner and go down, or be the animal knocked down (101).

She notes that Homer has "a habit, at mocking moments, of treating enemies as lovers, fusing the effects of Eros and Thanatos" (102, 157). So the brothers of Dinah unman the Shechemites through trickery that makes them unable to respond to the battle.

The same juxtaposition of "slaughter and sex" that Vermeule finds in Greek tradition is found in the tale of Jael, but here one of the soldiers, the one who wins, is actually a woman. The woman's role is thus markedly different from those of Dinah and the Timnite women. She is the center and heroine of the story. The woman confronts the warrior who came to battle in a chariot with a tent peg, a domestic fixture of her homelife, and in this way symbolizes the victory of the marginal over the publicly powerful. This duel by trickery that like the scenes studied by Vermeule takes place in "its own world, apart from the main battle" is a contest between the weak and the strong, in which the weak prevails. Here the weak one who prevails is a female, the marginal gender in Israel as tales of Dinah and the Timnite indicate.

The world-view that contrasts Israelite with "Other" and oppressed with oppressor and the war ideology that imagines victory through trickery are at work in the tale of Jael as in tales of Samson and the sons of Jacob. And once again, we are reminded how one group's noble warrior hero is its enemy's duplicitous assassin.

Ehud and Eglon: Judges 3:12–30

The setting as in the tale of Jael is Israel's subjugation by a non-Israelite power. Israel has been under the sway of Eglon, king of Moab, for eighteen years (Judg 3:13–14). The people cry out to God and he provides a savior, Ehud, a left-handed man. Ehud's left-handedness is the key to his trickster's defeat of Eglon. He hides his short double-edged sword on his right thigh, under his clothes—presumably most warriors would keep their swords on the left in order to draw easily with the right hand. He poses as an informant to the king and obtains a private audience with him; his hidden weapon is not discovered. When alone with the king, he says "I have a message from God for you," unleashes his sword with his left hand and kills Eglon, a man so obese that the fat closes over the blade after Ehud thrusts it in (3:22). The author thus paints a grisly portrait of the assassination of a literal "fat cat," Israel's oppressor, by a wily trickster who is appropriately left-handed—left being the marginal, less favored, underhanded side of the body in an Israelite symbol system. (See the use of the preferred right side in ritual contexts Ex 29:20, 22; Lev 7:32; 8:23, 25, etc. and contrast Eccl 10:2). With Eglon dead, the Israelites are able to rout the Moabites and gain liberation from them "for eighty years" (3:28–30).

Gary Anderson treats the scene of Eglon's assassination in his study of sacrifice in the Hebrew Scriptures as rich in the symbolism of ritual slaughter. Eglon whose name suggests the root of the word for calf is the "fatted calf" slaughtered as the "prelude to Israel's sacral war" (74; Alter, 1981:39). A Freudian interpreter of this scene might well find in it some of the same mixture of "slaughter" and "sex" that shapes the tale of Jael. (See the brief move in this direction by Alter, 1981:39.) The thigh is a place to hitch a sword (Ex 32:27; Song 3:8) but the thigh or loins is also the seat of male fertility (Gen 46:26; Ex 1:5). The short double-edged sword upon the thigh, hidden under clothing, is a strongly phallic image. Ehud tells the king that he has a secret for him. The word "secret" (though not the same term used in Judges 4) has connotations of intimacy. This term describes a conversation between political intimates Johanan and Gedaliah concerning a plotted assassination at Jer 40:15. Jeremiah is portrayed as a father confessor of sorts to King Zedekiah at Jer 37:17 and 38:16, passages in which the two men converse "in secret." The "in secret" phrase also, however, has qualities of enticement at Deut 13:6 [v. 7 in Hebrew] and Job 31:27 and describes David's adulterous liaison with Bathsheba at 2 Sam 12:12. Does the political once again intertwine with the sexual in the language and imagery of Ehud's tale? He thrusts the sword into Eglon. The same word is used for Jael's thrusting the tent peg at Judges 4:21. Eglon's fat closes over each side of the blade in a vaginal image of the lethal wound. Ehud locks the door and leaves. It is not stated whether his departure is observed or not.

The scene ends curiously with Eglon's retainers wondering what keeps him so long in the locked roof chamber. The Hebrew then offers a difficult phrase. Depending on the vocalization one chooses, they think to themselves that he is within, covering his "private parts" (literally his feet) which some scholars take to mean "moving the bowels because of the position assumed" (BDB; see also Halpern, 1988b:35 who makes a good case for this translation) or "pouring out his male member" in the roof-chamber, i.e. urinating in his water closet. NRSV, NEB, and Boling (1975) translate "relieving himself." "They waited until they were embarrassed. And still, he did not open the doors of the roof-chamber"; then they entered and found him dead (3:25). What did they think he was doing and what does that curious phrase involving private parts mean? Saul too enters a cave to engage in this idiom, the same cave where David and his men are hiding. David opts not to kill Saul while he is in this exposed position of vulnerability and instead cuts off a piece of his garment, a proof that he could have killed but did not (1 Sam 24:1–7). The severed piece of cloth also conjures images of unmanning the enemy. Thus are David's emissaries to the Ammonites shaved and their garments cut in half up to their "rear ends," an aggressive act that humiliates and feminizes David's messengers, leading to war and the Ammonites' own eventual subjugation (2 Sam 10:1–19; 1 Chron 19:1–19). Nuances of vulnerability, intimacy, sexuality, and death thus lurk in the language and imagery of Eglon's assassination.

Conclusions

All four tales are dominated by the contest between those occupying a marginal place in society and the powerful, those at the center of society with the capacity to oppress. Power is expressed in three, perhaps all four, passages in sexual terms. The underdogs wrest status from the "Other" through deception. Finally, the passages suggest that victory, even if for the long period of eighty years (Judges 3:30), is only temporary.

The enemy deserves to be killed because he is an oppressor. Just cause for war is found in the trickster war portrayals as in the ban as God's justice. Confrontation is not direct, however; it is necessarily sneaky. God, moreover, is absent in Genesis 34, absent in the tale of Jael in Judges 4 and 5, mentioned once by Ehud before he kills Eglon, and mentioned three times in the Samson tale 14:4, 19; 15:14 (God's "opportunity" and the divine war frenzy that comes over Samson). The context of these stories does assume God's control and presence, but the cameo scenes themselves pit human wit against the more powerful but less clever enemy. Odysseus-like, Huck Finn-like, these characters rely on their own resources to survive. While such tales of trickery certainly appeal to the underdog side of all of us and can be told in any period or setting, it does seem that they would appeal most to those outside the power structure. The ideology of war that emerges from tales of trickster warriors is most likely a popular ideology rather than a courtly one, while the tales themselves would have held special appeal to Israelite societies as a whole during their many periods of external political, economic, and cultural subjugation, which accounts for virtually the whole of Israel's history. The response to oppression differs significantly from the texts portraying banning wars for God's justice. Pragmatic, self-sufficient, and street-smart, this ideology is more realistic than others about the possibility of eliminating the sources of oppression and discord.

A More Respectable Tricksterism

The Book of Esther with its strongly ethnic pro-Jewish flavor and its jingoistic distrust of and disdain for foreigners has occasioned bouts of virulent anti-Judaism even on the part of respected, modern scholars. Singled out for particular condemnation are sections at 8:11, 9:5–6 in which the Jews are described as striking down their enemies with vehemence. In the bombastic repetitive style typical of the whole of the book, Esth 9:5–6 reads:

> And the Jews struck all their enemies, a slaughter by the sword, a killing, and an annihilation and they did to those who hated them as they pleased. In the citadel of Susa the Jews killed and annihilated five hundred.

Esth 8:11 echoes 3:13 in which under the influence of the evil counsellor Haman, the witless Persian ruler Ahasuerus issues a decree ordering the annihilation of all the Jews, "young and old, women and children," and the plundering of all their possessions. At Esth 8:11 comes the reversal. Queen Esther has intervened to save her people, and letters are issued allowing Jews to defend themselves. But how to translate the end of v. 11? Does it say that in just deserts the Jews may now kill their enemies and their wives and children or that they may defend themselves against those who were about to kill them (the Jews) including their (the Jews') wives and children. NEB opts for the former nuance, while RSV and NRSV leave the translation ambiguous like the Hebrew itself.

In any event, misunderstanding the full spectrum and complex chronology of war ideologies in the Hebrew Bible as well as failing to appreciate the traditional narrative pattern of the tale, scholars accuse the fifth-century BCE author of Esther of returning to a primitive ethic of war rich in bloodthirsty vengeance. In fact, the war ethic of Esther is much more nuanced than these critics allow, belonging to the tricksterism trajectory but a sort of tricksterism made more respectable, the tricksterism called "wisdom."

As in the trickster tales explored above, the heroes and heroines find themselves in a politically and culturally marginal position. The great empire of the Persians has replaced the Babylonians on the world-scene, now controlling Israel. Esther and her cousin Mordecai do not live in Israel, but are Jews living in Susa itself, exiles in the diaspora. Mordecai, in fact, is a part of the court bureaucracy, a counsellor to the King Ahasuerus. One of the wonderful folktale themes of the work tells how Esther, an orphan who had been adopted by her righteous and well-placed cousin, rises from obscurity to become queen, the king's favorite. Another equally traditional theme tells how Mordecai saves the king's life by uncovering a plot against him. The dominant theme of the narrative, however, involves the court contest between Mordecai and another foreign counsellor, an Agagite named Haman.

Haman resents Mordecai's refusal to bow down to him literally and symbolically and attempts to rid himself of his rival, a Jew, by going to the king, accusing all the Jews of Persia of rebellion against the crown, and persuading Ahasuerus to issue a decree for their destruction.

Mordecai/Esther and Haman personify wisdom and anti-wisdom respectively. And yet to be wise here does not necessarily mean to be absolutely honest. As in trickster tales, the wise person often succeeds through the clever and successful use of deception to achieve good ends. The fool, like Haman, also deceives but to no good end. He is destroyed because of his trickery and in the case of Haman because he is so hubristic and caught up in himself that he cannot tell when a deception is upon him.

Thus Haman is flattered when Queen Esther invites him to attend a banquet she has prepared for himself and the king, and again, as tension in the story builds, when she prepares a second banquet for them. Esther plies the king with food and drink and provides an opportunity for the king to behold and appreciate her womanly beauty. Overcome with the sensual pleasures offered by the queen, Ahasuerus extravagantly offers Esther anything she wishes, even up to half of his kingdom. Humbly, she asks for her life and that of her people and dramatically reveals that Haman, the other dinner guest, is her adversary. Like Jael and the second-century BCE character Judith, Esther uses the wiles of women to ensnare and defeat her enemy. Sensuality or sexuality is related to the deception as in the trickster tales discussed above. The marginals survive and succeed, their enemies killed.

The death of those who would have killed the heroes is, of course, a typical ending in this variety of underdog tale and an integral part of the war ideology of tricksterism in which those outside the center of power use whatever means necessary to overcome enemies, preserve status, or survive.

And yet Esther's tale differs from that of the tricksters. Esther and Mordecai are not entirely outside the center of power, but seek to be a part of it, to use their wisdom to manipulate the powerful and foolish king. Unlike the tricksters, they do not "burn their bridges behind them" by killing the tyrant. Theirs is not a political ethic of rebellion against those who hold power, but a form of "collaboration with tyranny." (Niditch, 1987:126–45. The phrase is that of David Daube.) They walk a political tightrope that allows them self-preservation but not independence. They hold considerable power when things go well at court but always face the threat of being deposed, scape-goated, and destroyed.

In contrast to the authors of the trickster tales, the author of Esther goes to great lengths to portray the Jews as good citizens. To overemphasize the Jews' just vengeance at 9:5–6 is to misunderstand completely the dominant messages of the narrative, namely, that Haman's accusations were completely false, that Mordecai was the king's most loyal counsellor who saved his very life, that Esther was the most naturally beautiful, humble, and subservient of the women at court. She is thus contrasted with the King's previous wife Vashti who was dismissed after refusing to appear before the king and his drunken companions. Indeed Vashti appeals more to us as feminists than Esther. The Book of Esther, however, is not about feminism if the latter be defined in part as a challenge to the subjugation of women in the business-as-usual, androcentric world. Esther gets her way through one of the means available to those out of power, by playing the system to her own advantage. The Book of Esther is not about rebellion. It is fascinating, in fact, not that the Jews kill their enemies but that they do so only after having been given written, legal permission by the king to defend themselves (see Esth 8:9–14). Moreover, they take no booty from their enemies (9:9). In the ban as God's justice, especially as invoked against Israelites, the denial of booty is to be understood in terms of fear of contagion from that which is idolatrous and unclean and in terms of guilt about profiting from the death of kin. In the ban as sacrifice, booty might be denied to Israelites as God's portion. Here, the denial of booty portrays the Jews as good citizens who do only what is necessary to defend themselves and survive. They are not in the war to benefit materially; they do not wish to wage war. By the same token, as in the trickster tales, no tell-tale sign of guilt about killing clouds their jubilation in victory, for as the song celebrating the holiday of Purim goes, "Haman is banished"—at least for the moment.

6

The Ideology of Expediency
and Biblical Critique

In his study of just and unjust wars, Michael Walzer points to William Tecumseh Sherman's famous dictum, "War is hell" (1977:32–33; 204n.; 230; 265). This view of war implies that there is no use in contemplating codes or restrictions on the killing, certainly no point in fooling oneself that war can be fought nobly or ignobly, adhering to or ignoring *jus in bello*. The cause may well be just—surely Sherman believed in the survival of the union—but once war begins, the best one can do is to fight efficiently and pragmatically, to do, in short, whatever is necessary to win as decisively and quickly as possible. If civilians are killed along the way, so be it; if striking terror into the hearts of one's enemy by barbarism is helpful to one's goals, so be it. The particular rationalizations for killing implicit in the ban-as-sacrifice tradition, the ban as God's justice, and the priestly ideology of Numbers 31 have no place in the biblical version of "war as hell," nor do the self-glorifying heroic views of combat found in the bardic tradition. This pragmatic, war-is-hell point of view does not stem from the powerless who are unable to fight "efficiently" in this sense. The "war-is-hell" ideology belongs to the powerful, able to use professional force to impose their will upon those perceived as the enemy.

An Opening Case: The Critique
of Naked Aggression

Judges 9 describes one of the northern Israelite bandit chiefs' attempts to establish a monarchy in the style of the various small, petty tyrannies of the ancient Near East. Abimelech, a son of the hero Gideon (also called Jerubbaal) by a Shechemite concubine, is said to hold power for three years, but the "lords of Shechem" rebel against him. The biblical narrator, in fact, frames their rebellion in terms of just vengeance, for Abimelech had come to power by murdering his opponents, all his own kin "the sons of Jerubbaal." The narrator thus firmly rejects such uses of aggression by those with the power to grab what they want, especially when the aggression is directed at kinfolk. Abimelech appears to beat back the challenge by the Shechemites. He captures the city, kills the people in it, demolishes the city and sows it with salt (Judg 9:45). Finally he sets on fire the Tower of Shechem, the stronghold where "a thousand men and women" had taken refuge (9:49). Abimelech's career of conquest ends in a battle against Thebez when a woman who had fled to its Tower throws down a millstone and crushes his head, a favorite way in Hebrew Scriptures to end the lives of oppressors (cf. Judg 4:21, 5:24-27).

This passage provides an interesting entrance to the study of the war ideology of expediency. In it a man who would acquire power and control of territory takes it upon himself to murder, strafe, and burn his way to victory. Implicit in the tale of his eventual failure is a critique of this ideology. Significantly, his reign of terror has not been justified or blessed by God. In many other passages, those holding power are just as materialist, self-serving, and brutal as Abimelech, but are regarded as having divine sanction.

The Usual Literary Pattern of State-Sponsored War

The recurring literary patterns in which such wars of the powerful are imagined create a more orderly and controlled phenomenon than any reality of war; such imaginings nevertheless reveal some of their authors' beliefs and assumptions about war.

The Israelite king often requests an oracle from God concerning the battle, advice is given and followed, the Israelite troops are victorious, the enemy is killed or enslaved, booty is taken, and the matter settled in Israel's favor. Some or all of these motifs are found in David's confrontation with the Philistines and others (2 Sam 5:17-25 = 1 Chron 14:8-17; 2 Sam 8:1-13; 1 Sam 23:1-5) and in wars with the Ammonites and Aramaeans at 2 Sam 10:6-19 (see also 1 Chron 18-19) and 2 Sam 12:26-31 = 1 Chron 20:1-3. (For ancient Near Eastern parallels and further discussion see Kang:56-72; 98-107; 215-222.)

In Israel as in the ancient Near East as a whole, the support of the deity is deemed necessary for victory; victory is indication of the god's favor and power as defeat is indication of his/her disfavor or impotence. This basic assumption about God's power expressed in portrayals of wars of expedience thus does not differ from one essential belief underlying each of the ideologies explored above.

A Case of Claiming Just Cause

While the ideology of expediency does not attempt to make excuses for massive killing in war, as we have argued the ban texts implicitly do, and while no code limiting the killing is found as in the bardic tradition, a few portrayals that treat war as business-as-usual, the frequent activity of the state, nevertheless claim just cause for going to war. In these cases, the outcome of the war is deemed to reveal divine judgment concerning which side's cause was the more just. The war thus becomes a trial of sorts.

The prelude to Jephthah's battle with the Ammonites in Judges 11 is important in this regard. Jephthah sends a message to the king of the Ammonites, "What is there between myself and you that you come to me to fight against my land?" (11:12). Note that Jephthah's very language lays claim to the land. The Ammonite responds that Israel had taken away his land in coming forth from Egypt, and asks that Jephthah return it in peace. The author thus portrays a territorial dispute based on Israel's own foundation myth. Jephthah responds with a lengthy recounting of Israel's early journey to the land (not all of which is frankly relevant to the dispute at hand). He seems to claim that Israel's conquest was not illegal or unethical. Because Edom, Moab, and the Ammonites would not let Israel pass peacefully, Israel had to conquer the disputed territory. The defense at v. 21 is somewhat different: God had given this land to his people. Let the Ammonites keep what their god Chemosh had given them to possess, and Israel what Yahweh had given them. Divine promises to each side are thus reflected in recognized borders as they now stand. Belief in the god's capacity to bestow rights to land becomes not an encouragement for conquest, but a means of justifying and upholding the current territorial status quo. This is a fascinating passage, so different in its use of the conquest tradition than the Deuteronomic collection explored in chapter 2.

Finally at Judg 11:26, Jephthah lays claim to the area on the basis of Israel's long-term undisputed settlement in the area: Israel has lived in all the towns along the Ammon for three hundred years. Why has Ammon not attempted to "liberate" them (literally "to save") in all that time?

The sides cannot reach agreement and the war proceeds, but the plea to just cause is very sophisticated, the concern with political ethics stunning. Jephthah states "I have not sinned against you, but you do me wrong to fight against me. Let the Lord, the judge, decide today between the people of Israel and the people of Ammon" (11:27). Thus wars require just causes and to fight without just cause is to do evil. The group whose cause is just will prevail.

The assurance that the side with just cause will achieve victory is not sufficient to prevent Jephthah from promising a sacrifice to God in v. 29 should he win, a sacrifice which turns out to be his own daughter. Is he bribing the divine judge?

Judges 11:29 appears to begin a new story and presents a war ideology that includes vowing human beings to God (see chapter 1), an ideology different in interest and concern from that of Jephthah's case to the Ammonites. It is, however, interesting to see how various war ideologies can coexist in literature—perhaps also in life. The ideology allowing for war-vows that may involve human sacrifice is, after all, also a pragmatic ideology of sorts. One does whatever is necessary to win the war. What Judges 11 says in its current form is the war should not be entertained unless it is just.

Expedient Wars without Just Cause or Code

The vast majority of texts that display a pragmatic and expedient attitude to war, however, do not concern themselves with matters of just cause and certainly not with codes for conduct in fighting, nor do they evidence guilt concerning the killing their wars perpetrate. Instead rulers are portrayed who seek to exploit land, goods, and people to assert, maintain, and increase their power. This is not to say they do not believe or at least declare for public consumption that the powers of the divine realm are in favor of their warring actions. Thus the Assyrian Rabshakeh says to King Hezekiah (2 Kings 18:25) "Now, is it without Yahweh that I have come against this place to destroy it? Yahweh said to me, 'Go up against that land and destroy it.'" In clever propaganda, delivered in a rhetorical tour de force, he tells those he hopes to defeat that their own God is against them. With God's help the pragmatists make war as is necessary and desirable to further political, territorial, and economic goals.

Ecological Materialism in Earnest and Up-Front

Anthropologists of a Marxian or cultural materialist persuasion suggest that ideologies such as the ban as God's justice, in fact, mask the true goals of combat and killing in war—namely the desire to take the enemy's land or goods or women in order better to assure the prospering, perhaps the very survival, of one's own group. We have sought to understand the banning and other ideologies of war more complexly as expressions of varying cultural threads in ancient Israel and in terms of human responses toward manifestations of the "Other," asking how people react to and employ violence, power, and oppression.

The passages characterized by the expedient ideology, however, wear materialist causes for war overtly. Josh 19:47 tells of the Danites' need for land. The Hebrew is difficult at this point, reading either that they had lost their territory or that they found themselves pushing beyond their borders. It says literally "the boundary of Dan went from them." They rise up, fight with the inhabitants of a town named Leshem, and conquer it, putting everyone to the sword, renaming the town Dan, and claiming it as their inheritance. The language of "striking with the edge of the sword," familiar from ban texts, here receives none of the ideological framework of the ban. Another even more interesting tale of Dan's formative exploits is found at Judg 18:7-13, 27-31. The Danites go to Laish whose inhabitants are described as an isolated, peaceful, quiet people living after the manner of the Sidonians, lacking nothing in the land, keeping to themselves. Announcing to one another how good this land is (18:9-10), the Danites summarily declare it God's gift to them, gird on their war gear, acquire a priest for themselves along the way and "strike them (the Laishians) with the sword and burn their city with fire" (18:27). "There was no savior, for it (Laish) was far from Sidon and they had no intercourse with anyone" (Judg 18:28). The narrator repeats over and over how peaceful and trusting are the Laishians (18:7, 10, 27). Does he want to emphasize simply that they are a good target for conquest, the point of view of the protagonists he creates, or is he implicitly critical of such unadorned aggression? In any event, the ideology of the war of expedience is illustrated by these Danite founding myths. Some scholars seek history in such tales, information about some of the groups that later came together to form Israel, or some sense of the way an early Israelite occupation of the land might have taken place. The tales of the Danites cannot yield such information, but they are fine examples of the ideology of wars of expedience, a variety that eschews any need for just cause (compare Jephthah's case above).

Similar brief references to such conquests are found at Num 32:39-42, the key verb used in these texts being "to capture"/"to siege." 1 Kings 9:16 describes Pharaoh's emptying out of Gezer in order to give it to his daughter as dowry when she marries King Solomon. Again, the city is burned, the people killed in language found in ban passages, but the ethic is entirely different. If one has the power, one can use it for one's own benefit.

Dead People Cannot Fight (or Tell Secrets)

Some of the massive killing reminiscent of the totality of the ban is for equally pragmatic reasons. One tries to eliminate as many of the enemy as possible for strategic purposes (see Daly and Wilson: 232-

33 on the so-called "fitness" argument for massive killing—more of "you" will survive if you kill all of "them"). At 1 Kings 11:15–16, Joab, David's army commander, is said to have killed "every male in Edom." He spends six months in the reign of terror, until he "cuts off every male in Edom" (1 Kings 11:16) (though in the next breath, the narrator announces that some had escaped). The killings are apparently not in vengeance, nor merely to strike terror in David's would-be enemies, but to eliminate one of Israel's foes.

Similarly, while a vassal to Achish the Philistine, David, a bandit chief at this point in his career, makes raids upon local non-Israelite communities, taking away their animals and clothing. He kills all human beings, but again not as sacrifices to God or in a banning as a war of God's justice. In order to win the trust of the Philistines, David has told his overlord that the raids have been against his own people. David must kill the non-Judean objects of his raids in order to leave no witnesses (1 Sam 27:9–11). "David did not allow a man or woman to live to be brought to Gath, thinking 'Lest they inform upon us saying, "Thus did David do"'" (1 Sam 27:11). The killing is not ordered by God, not just vengeance, but a pragmatic act necessary for David to maintain his position and perhaps his life.

Brutality in War and the Aftermath

The most unsettling aspect of passages that belong to the expedient trajectory is the naked brutality with which enemies are treated. The barbarism of King Menachem of Israel is described at 2 Kings 15:16: "At this time Menachem struck Tiphsah and all that was in it . . . because it did not open (to him), he ripped open all its pregnant women."

David, considered by the ongoing tradition to be the ideal leader of the Hebrew Scriptures, is described as a skilled practitioner of the biblical war-is-hell ideology. A strange little passage about the conquest of Jerusalem relates as follows:

> The king and his men came to Jerusalem against the Jebusites, the inhabitants of the land, and they said to David, "You will not enter here, for even the blind and the lame will repel you. David will not enter here!" (2 Sam 5:6).

The Jebusites greet David with a taunt. Even a cripple could beat you! Do they perhaps believe their sacred city to be impregnable? Isaiah would make the same claim about Jerusalem, his people's holy city, but it is destroyed by Nebuchadnezzar some two hundred years later. Such declarations buoy up the confidence of those who face aggression. Within the belief systems of Israel and its neighbors, such statements anticipating victory or salvation are moreover regarded as having self-fulfilling power. Perhaps David indicates his own belief in the efficacy of the Jebusites' words or his fear of them in what follows:

> David captured the stronghold of Zion, that is the City of David. And David declared on that day, "Let everyone who would strike the Jebusites, strike . . . the lame and the blind, the enemies of the soul of David. For this reason they say "The blind and the lame shall not enter the Temple" (2 Sam 5:7-8).

A biblical author, himself uncomfortable with the tradition, treats it as an etiology for a saying concerning fitness to enter the holy temple in Jerusalem.

David is portrayed, however, as cruel and vengeful, answering the taunt of those he would conquer by striking down the defenseless members of their society who are surely not responsible for having been used in a taunt. To use unnecessary force, exceeding requirements for winning even the most materialist of wars, is the antithesis of *jus in bello*. This passage paints a contrast in ideology with the bardic and related traditions. The efficacy in such killing is that it strikes fear into all opponents, making future resistance less likely. It is a strategy of the tyrant. Nor does this narrative provide an isolated portrait of David as monarch. The king's treatment of Moabite prisoners is described in 2 Sam 8:2. Having defeated Moab, David makes the prisoners lie down on the ground and measures them with a chord length. Two lengths' worth he condemns to death, one length's worth he allows to live. Some have explained this passage by suggesting that David kills the tallest and ablest men, allowing the runts to live as if David were employing genetic selection to weaken Moabite stock. In fact, David is pictured to be coldly more arbitrary, claiming for himself the godly power of life and death. The treatment of prisoners provides a means of establishing total control over enemies, of melting their hearts in terror of the fearless and guiltless way with which the tyrant takes life. Again, the contrast with passages such as 2 Kings 6:20–23 is stunning (see chapter 4 above).

In a comparable fashion, under King Amaziah of Judah the people of Judah are said to kill ten thousand men of Seir and to take another ten thousand live. They bring these captives to the top of Sela and throw them down alive so that they are "smashed to pieces," literally "split apart," by the fall (2 Chron 25:11–12).

Booty in Goods and People

As in the bardic or heroic tradition, the acquisition of booty is a major goal of the wars of expediency. At times the booty is dedicated to God (2 Sam 8:11–12). At other times it contributes to the victor's aggrandizement.

After defeating Rabbah the royal city of Ammon, David takes the crown of Milcom, the national deity of the Ammonites, from upon his head—such a crowned statue would have been a symbol of the local deity's indwelling presence and kingship (McCarter, 1984:312–13)—and places the jeweled and golden crown upon his own head (2 Sam 12:30 = 1 Chron 20:2). David thus assumes the foreign deity's status and power, for in traditional cultures you are what you wear (2 Sam 12:30). He also takes much booty (12:30) and sets the people at forced labor (on problems in the translation of 2 Sam 12:31 see McCarter, 1984: 311, 313).

This passage provides a startling contrast with the ideology of the ban as God's justice in which the enemy's worship-related booty is absolutely forbidden, contaminated by its association with the worship of other gods. Here David is pictured not only to keep the crown but to assume the pose of the idol itself. The implicit worldview could not be more different from that of the ban as God's justice (see also 2 Sam 8:6–8 and especially the version in 1 Chron 18:3–7).

Finally in the ideology of expediency, the enemy's booty not only serves one's own enrichment but is the means by which the ruler can attract and hold allies. Thus after David defeats the Amalekites, he distributes part of the booty to "the elders of Judah, to his friends saying 'Here is a present for you from the booty of the enemies of

Yahweh'" (1 Sam 30:26). This is a pragmatic use of conquered goods appropriate to a war ideology of expedience.

Implicit Critique: The Work of the Chronicler

This chapter opened with the tale of Abimelech's brief career as a king who had come to power by a naked application of the ideology of expediency. The tale of Abimelech in Judges is shaped as a critique of that ideology or at least of that ideology when the aggression is directed at kin and not sanctioned by God.

Additional criticism of the brutality that often accompanies the ideology of expediency is found implicitly in the work of the Chronicler. The Books of 1 and 2 Chronicles provide a second version of the history of the kings of Israel. The material in 1 and 2 Chronicles is, in part, a rewrite of the Deuteronomic History, for large portions of 1 and 2 Chronicles are identical to sections of 2 Samuel, 1 and 2 Kings. The Chronicles traditions have added materials, some of which may come from early sources, and have reshaped accounts found in the Deuteronomic Corpus. 1 and 2 Chronicles raise complex issues in ancient Israelite historiography. Did its authors, for example, expect their work to take the place of the Deuteronomic History? Is their history writing preserving a view of the past (if not the actual past) or, more consciously, are the authors creating the past to suit their own times?

As the Deuteronomic Corpus was composed, in part, to present Israelite history in a way supportive of the Josianic reform and then later revised, so some scholars believe that 1 and 2 Chronicles was composed in support of a restoration movement by Judeans who returned from exile to the land with the permission of Persia (ca. 538 BCE). The restoration involved rebuilding the temple that had been destroyed in 586 BCE, an important leadership role for the Jerusalem Zadokite priesthood, and the reestablishment of a Davidic monarch on the throne. The temple is rebuilt between 520 and 515 BCE, the date suggested for the earliest portions of 1 and 2 Chronicles. This work too is revised reaching final form around 400 BCE (Cross, 1975; for a review of theories on the redaction history of 1 and 2 Chronicles, see McKenzie, 1985:1–32). A role for the Davidic monarch quickly fades from the Judean scene. The first restored monarch Zerubbabel is described in veritably messianic terms by the sixth-century prophets Zechariah and Haggai (Zechariah 4; 6:9–14; Hag 2:20–23). The Persians who had replaced the Babylonians as conquerors in control of Israel may well have abandoned support for the monarchy because of its potential to rally Israelites to rebel. Even in its current form, however, 1 and 2 Chronicles is extremely pro-Davidic.

For our purposes it is most interesting to examine what the Chroniclers have edited out of the stories of David. While the heroic tales of David and his men of valor are preserved pretty much in the form of the Deuteronomic History, portrayals of David as practitioner of the war ideology of expediency have been virtually expurgated. Thus the passage about eliminating the lame and blind during the conquest of Jerusalem (2 Sam 5:6–10) is eliminated in the parallel place in Chronicles' version of David's exploits (1 Chron 11:4–8). In this version, the taunt of the Jebusites is simplified to "You will not enter here." The reference to the lame and blind is nowhere to be found. Instead, in a manly way more reminiscent of the bardic tradition, David declares that "Whoever strikes the Jebusites first will be made a chief and commander." Similarly David's arbitrary and terror-inspiring treatment of the prisoners at 2 Sam 8:2 is completely left out at 1 Chron 18:2 where the victory over the Moabites is cited in abbreviated form.

The Chronicler does not want to portray David as a monarch who practices brutality as a regular feature of acquiring and holding power. As 1 Chron 11:9 concludes, "David kept growing greater and greater for the Lord of Hosts was with him." David is helped by God in his quest, not by the darker side of his humanity. Implicit in this positive view of David is a critique of the use of brutality in war. The Chronicler does not by any means eliminate all references to this sort of war ideology. Indeed Amaziah's forces look more cruel at 2 Chron 25:11–16 than at 2 Kings 14:7. The latter does not include throwing prisoners to their deaths on the rocks. The fact that David must be shielded from a portrayal as a practitioner of the brutality of expediency, however, clearly implies the Chronicler's discomfort with it. Indeed it is 1 Chron 22:8 that pictures David declaring that God himself told him not to build the holy temple in Jerusalem because he had shed so much blood in his many wars.

7

Toward an Ideology
of Nonparticipation

The Hebrew Scriptures allude to peace, its writers no less desirous
of an end to violence and war than any of us. The beautiful oracle
imagining a day when all wars have ceased, found in the eighth-
century BCE prophets Isaiah and Micah, testifies to this desire.

> They will beat their swords into plowshares,
> their spears into pruning hooks.
> Nation will not raise sword against nation,
> they will not continue to learn about war.
>   (Isa 2:4; Mic 4:3)

This prophecy, however, is set far in the future, "at the end of days"
(Mic 4:1; Isa 2:2). Only then can one expect disarmament, a life of
agrarian plenty, nonaggression among former enemies—generations not schooled in war. The reality acknowledged by biblical
writers of all periods differs.

Domination versus Reconciliation

Many scholars have noted that for ancient Israelite authors, peace,
the state of shalom, also implied Israel's dominance over all nations
who might threaten her and often their coming to accept Israel's own
world-view and her God (e.g. Zech 8:20–23). Thus Pedersen notes,

In the olden time peace is not in itself the opposite of war. There are friends and there are enemies; peace consists in complete harmony between friends and victory in the war against enemies . . . (Vol. 1, 311).

Citing passages such as Judges 8:7–9; 2 Sam 19:24, 30 (vv. 25, 31 in the Hebrew); 1 Kgs 22:28; and Jer 43:12, Pedersen suggests that peace is not merely the "release from fighting," enjoyed at last by victors and vanquished alike, but a state-of-being experienced only by the winning side (Vol. 1, 312).

(God) will come and strike the land of Egypt.
To death, he who is to die.
To captivity, he who is to be captive.
To the sword, he who is for the sword.
He will kindle a fire
in all the temples of the gods of Egypt,
burn them and capture them.
He will wrap up the land of Egypt
like a shepherd wraps up his robe.
And he will go forth from there in peace.
(Jer 43:11,12)

With an oracle intoning the quality of incantation the enemy is doomed to death or enslavement, his holy places to devastation, and his land to conquest. In this setting comes Yahweh's peace. It is a chilling juxtaposition, cascading images of war and a single phrase, taking only three words in the Hebrew, describing God's peace.

Pedersen is perhaps too sweeping in his insistence that peace is virtually equivalent to domination. Nuances of healing and unification between former enemies are not completely absent from the Hebrew Scriptures. At Judges 21:13, for example, the winners of the civil war between the tribe of Benjamin and the other tribes "proclaim peace" to their former enemies. This phrase could be interpreted to mean that the non-Benjaminites declare themselves victorious, but Judg 21:14 goes on to show means by which the victors hope to achieve genuine reconciliation, namely by offering their former enemies women-spoil. Women thus serve in a typical role assigned them by biblical writers and Israelite culture as transition-makers, connectors, and items of exchange between opposing groups. In any event, a peace between equals is established.

The words put into the mouth of an elderly King David at 1 Kgs 2:5 are also interesting in this context. David, soon to die, gives parting advice to his son Solomon. He asks Solomon to seek vengeance against Joab, the general who had served him so long but who had killed David's beloved son Absalom when the latter sought to overthrow him. David's enmity toward Joab is unfair and deeply rooted in his own feelings of guilt and denial concerning a rebellious and disloyal son. The family history of David is a fine, psychologically complex work worthy of William Faulkner's interest in it. Here, however, David justifies his wish for the death of Joab in terms relevant for definitions of war and peace. David accuses Joab of "setting" (Hebrew manuscript tradition) or of "taking vengeance for" (a Greek manuscript tradition) "the blood of war during peace-time." There is thus a time of peace and a time of war. War-blood has to be forgotten once peace-time comes.

Granted, each of the above passages has to do with internicene strife within Israel. Pedersen might say that "friends" have temporarily fallen out during such states of war and reconciliation mends the unfortunate fissure. Nevertheless, relations between Israelites can provide a model of reconciliation for less closely related opponents in war as seen in the treatment of foreign prisoners in 2 Kgs 6:22–23 (see chapter 4).

A Critique of War?

Is there, however, a biblical war ideology that is critical of war itself and of people's participation in the taking of life that is a part of war?

We have mentioned Hosea's condemnation of Jehu's excesses (Hos 1:4) that may be read as a criticism of ban-like activities and the tale of Abimelech's rise and fall (Judges 9) that may be read as a challenge to the ideology of expediency. A plea for fair treatment of prisoners of war is implicit in 2 Kgs 6:20–23.

Certain threads of the ideologies discussed in chapters 1–7 also may be interpreted as critical of war. The banning traditions, violent and bloody as they are, reveal ways in which humans try to distance themselves from responsibility for the killing. Each of the banning ideologies admits of a process of rationalization that implies guilt within the human soul and therefore the potential for critique. The ideology of the ban as God's justice, in particular, seeks to justify killing in a vituperative, self-conscious way that shouts of self-doubt. The description of the end of civil war in Judges 21:1–11 may be an implicit critique of the ban when that ideology becomes an excuse to kill and conquer. The ritual cleansing and guilt offering necessary after war in Numbers 31 may well also admit of guilt concerning killing in war. Participation in the death of other human beings tears the social fabric asunder and makes impossible communion with God. Paradoxically, even a war of punishment commanded by God himself is unclean-rendering. Ritual means are necessary to heal the warriors and their conquests, to allow again for proper functioning of the sacred and the profane. The bardic tradition is characterized by a code limiting the form and conduct of war and provides a model for a more secular just-war tradition. And yet, at a conscious level these traditions accept killing in war as necessary (ban as sacrifice), desirable (ban as God's justice), or cause for glory (bardic tradition). The ban as God's justice and bardic traditions indeed encourage participation in war whatever the unconscious sense of guilt that leads to claims of justification in the one case and honorable limits in the other. The ideology of expediency implies no critique of killing in war, though its very existence may evoke such a critique in us either as disinterested readers or as more conscious participants in the western, biblically generated traditions of war.

Overt Critiques of Warring Behavior
in Gen 49 and Amos 1-2

In an interesting example of inner-biblical dialogue, Gen 49:5–7 alludes critically to the story of the rape of Dinah (Genesis 34) and implicitly to the tale's ideology of tricksterism. This difficult-to-date-and-place piece of tradition (Westermann; 1986:221) is part of the so called "Blessings of Jacob," a final testament of the aged patriarch who is pictured to address each of his sons. Simeon and Levi's slaying of men in anger and willful hamstringing of oxen (49:6) is decried as unfair and inappropriate: "Cursed be their anger, for it is fierce / Their overflowing rage, for it is relentless."

The interest of the writer who placed this saying in its biblical context is probably less in the ethics of war than in explaining aspects of the tribes' status in Israel, especially Levi's lack of a tribal holding. Nevertheless, Gen 49:5–7 provides a fascinating ideological counterpoint to Genesis 34, a view of warring behavior more in tune with the bardic code than with the marginal's tricksterism.

A more extended and self-consciously critical treatment of aspects of warring behavior is found in Amos 1–2. These chapters contain a series of indictments of Israel's neighboring states that culminates dramatically in a ringing condemnation of the kingdoms Judah and Israel themselves. The "transgressions" of Israel's neighbors, Damascus, Philistia, Ammon, Moab, Tyre, and Edom, involve the conduct of war. While some scholars accept all sections of this series as the work of the eighth century BCE prophet (see most recently Paul:61, 65; Polley:57, 75–82), others, for reasons of form and content, consider the oracles against Tyre (1:9–10) and Edom (1:11–12) as secondary additions of the sixth century BCE (Wolff, 1977:158, 160; see the discussion of Mays, 1969:34, 35–36).

Within the formulaic numerical patterning that frames the condemnations ("For three transgressions / For four"), the neighboring states are accused not only of daring to wage war against God's people, but of excesses in war. Gaza and Tyre have enslaved and sold off entire communities (1:6, 9). Tyre is accused moreover of not upholding treaty obligations (1:9). Edom is condemned for waging war against kin (1:11), that is, against Jacob or Israel, brother of Esau (Edom) in the genealogical tradition. NRSV and others translate a portion of Edom's wrongdoings listed in 1:11 as "he (Edom) cast off all pity," literally "destroyed brotherly compassion," from the Hebrew root *rḥm*. Shalom Paul, however, creatively translates "destroyed his womenfolk" (43), reading the *rḥm* term found also in Judg 5:30 as a reference to women, related to the root meaning womb. In addition, Edom, like Simeon and Levi in Genesis 49, is condemned for perpetual anger, eternal wrath (1:11). In particular, the oracle against the Ammonites criticizes the conduct of and the frequent cause for wars of expediency; the Ammonites have "ripped open pregnant women of Gilead in order to widen their borders" (1:13).

The Book of Amos thus offers a powerful critique of the ideology of expediency. Territorial gain is not just cause for the tactics of terror. Treaties are to be honored, war against kin is improper, excessive fury in the fighting and massive enslavement of prisoners are deemed wrong. Like the bardic tradition, the oracles in Amos 1-2 express apparent approval of the idea of limiting war, e.g. against women and kin, and evidence a quite conscious if brief reflection on reasons for fighting, conduct of war, and treatment of the defeated enemy.

1 and 2 Chronicles and War

1 and 2 Chronicles provide a more extended critique of human participation in the violence of war and a potential for an ideology of non-participation. As discussed in chapter 6, 1 and 2 Chronicles took shape during the period of Persian domination in the years from the rebuilding of the Temple (ca. 520 BCE) to ca. 400 BCE. This corpus exists in a special relationship to Samuel and Kings, much of which it parallels and reshapes; a good deal is to be learned about attitudes to war in 1 and 2 Chronicles from its particular additions to and deletions from the earlier corpus.

The omission of David's cruel actions as a leader practicing the war ideology of expediency is marked (see chapter 6). This is not to say that all such actions are eliminated from 1 and 2 Chronicles. It is 2 Chron 25:12 that describes Judeans throwing ten thousand enemy prisoners from a precipice to their deaths on the rocks and 2 Kgs 14:7 that includes a much briefer and cleaner version of King Amaziah's victory, eliminating the killing of the ten thousand. But the fact that David is not pictured to engage in these acts of terror is important, implying that the author regarded such acts of war to be unseemly, indecent, and not befitting the ideal leader. The Chronicler goes further in a peaceful direction in describing the ideal leader. Even David, his hero, is disqualified from building the holy Temple in Jerusalem because he was a warrior who had killed in battle. 2 Sam 7:1-29 (= 1 Chron 17:1-27) explains that David wanted to build the Temple, and God informed him in a dream that not he, but his son, reigning after him, would do so. In 1 Chron 22:7-10 and at 28:3 David is shown to expand the report of this divinely sent message.

David said to Solomon his son "It was in my heart to build a house for the name of Yahweh my God, but the word of Yahweh came upon me saying, 'Much blood you have shed, and great wars you have waged. You will not build a house for my name because you have shed so much blood on the ground before me. Behold a son will be born to you. He will be a man of peace and I will give him respite from all his enemies round about, for Solomon will be his name, and peace and quiet I will bestow upon Israel in his days. He will build a house for my name . . .'" (1 Chron 22:7-10).

Great and heroic as David is, ethical and godly, even in the conduct of war, he is not allowed to build God's holy dwelling on earth, the place where God's name will rest, because he has shed blood in battle. However noble and necessary the cause, the killing has disqualified him from constructing the sacred space. We are reminded of the connection between killing, death, and uncleanness in Numbers 31:19. Playing on the etymology of Solomon's name, *shelomo*, rooted in the word for peace, shalom, the divine message asserts that the man of peace will build the temple. He has not been sullied by the blood of war. (Compare the interpretation by Gabriel:67-72.)

The Chronicler and Crusade

It is interesting in this context that the Chronicler makes little mention of the conquest tradition. The work's opening genealogies schematize Israel's early history—in fact, the history of mankind from Adam until the death of Saul—in a way that makes Israel's presence in the land an eternal and inevitable verity. Mention of much of the bloodiest war traditions are in this way avoided. Even small details of phrasing may be revealing. 1 Kgs 9:20-21 refers to the Canaanites living in the land in the time of Solomon as follows: "All the nations remaining . . . that the people of Israel were not able to place under the ban." 2 Chron 8:7-8 states instead, "All the nations remaining . . . that the people of Israel did not put an end to." The former text implies that Israel sought to exterminate all the inhabitants of the land whereas the latter eliminates reference to the ban or Israel's volition and refers more simply to a less than complete conquest. The crusading aspect is lessened. Similarly

Jehu's purge, a lengthy bloody story about the prophetically supported annihilation of worshippers of the Canaanite god Baal and the Israelite royal house of Ahab sympathetic to them (2 Kgs 9:1–10:36), is reduced to a few verses in 2 Chronicles 22:7–9. The Chronicler should approve of the vengeance of God wreaked by Jehu, and 2 Chronicles does state that Jehu was anointed by the Lord to destroy the house of Ahab, but having said so cuts the tale of violence short.

It should not be concluded that 1 and 2 Chronicles lacks the crusading spirit. It is 2 Chron 15:13 and not the parallel place in 1 Kings 15 that has all the people of Judah and like-minded Yahwists from the north unite to take an oath—a covenant that "anyone who does not seek the Lord, God of Israel, should be put to death, whether small or grown-up, man or woman." The chain of those condemned rings with the sound of the ban texts and yet no purge is carried out, the assumption being perhaps that the threat and the act of self-dedication are sufficient to keep people in line. Also found in the account of 2 Chronicles and not in 1 Kings is the conclusion to the story of self-reformation, "And there was no war until the thirty-fifth year of the reign of Asa" (2 Chron 15:19; see also v. 15). Obedience to Yahweh brings peace. (For a full discussion of the Chroniclers' portrayals of war in terms of a system of divine retribution and human trial see Japhet:191–98.) This, again, is an ancient biblical theme particularly popular in the Deuteronomic corpus with its emphasis on blessings and curses, but the linkage of the absence of war with the vow to kill those unfaithful to God is a peculiar and potentially jarring one. That is, one might assume that such a vow would be followed by an outburst of violence. The writer, however, offers an ideal in which threats of death exist, but need not be carried out. The internal peace assured by faithfulness to God, in turn, is paralleled by release from one's non-Israelite enemies. God rewards faithfulness with peace (see also 2 Chron 17:7–10).

Peace as Victory in War

One should not overenthusiastically point to the emphasis on peace in 1 and 2 Chronicles. In Chronicles as elsewhere in the

Hebrew Bible, peace often implies the brutal subjugation of enemies (e.g. 1 Chron 22:18); even wars against fellow Israelites can
result in divinely sanctioned "great slaughter" (2 Chron 13:17)
carried out by the side that has God's support (2 Chron 13:12).
Certainly wars against non-Israelites can result in extermination
and pillaging of the enemy as the defeat of hordes of invading
Ethiopians indicates (2 Chron 14:9–15 [vv. 8–14 in the Hebrew]).
Offensive wars also can be successful if sanctioned as in wars of
Uzziah against the Philistines, Arabs, and Meunites at 2 Chron
26:6–15, military episodes not mentioned in the Deuteronomic
history.

Just as surely as divine support results in victory, divine disapproval leads to certain defeat as experienced by Ahaz (2 Chron
28:5) and Joash (2 Chron 24:23–24). The account of the latter's
confrontation with Hazael of Aram in 2 Kgs 12:18–19 is realistic in
its portrayal of ancient Near Eastern realpolitik. Hazael is bought
off by Joash (Jehoash) of Judah, who gives Hazael all the gold in
the treasuries of the Temple and other gifts amassed by his kingly
predecessors. After the pay-off, Hazael turns away from Jerusalem.
In 2 Chron 24:23–24, however, Joash is said to be defeated in battle
even though the enemy had come with few men and Joash had had
the larger, stronger force. The reason for this defeat is that the
Judeans had "forsaken the Lord, God of their fathers." Even the
good reforming king Josiah meets his death because he would not
listen to God's words not to fight against Neco of Egypt (2 Chron
35:20). Fantastically, the oracle from God is delivered by Neco
himself to whom God had spoken (2 Chron 35:21–22). The Chronicler does not pause to comment on the recurring problem in
biblical theodicy and prophecy concerning the identification of a
true message from God. In any event, God's presence and his
approval or disapproval of military encounters are constants in 1
and 2 Chronicles.

The writers of Chronicles are indeed more consistent than the
Deuteronomic historians in invoking the blessings-and-curses theology in regard to the outcome of wars. Speeches are put in the mouth
of Judean leaders before the wars, expounding on this theme of God
is on our side (2 Chron 32:8; 2 Chron 20:20). Commentaries or
postscripts are provided citing God's lack of support to explain
defeats (2 Chron 28:5; 2 Chron 24:24). God is in the battle listening to

the cries of his faithful to save them. Thus at 1 Kgs 22:32, the Judean king Jehoshaphat is spared when he cries out and the enemy realizes he is not King Ahab the leader whom they seek to kill. At 2 Chron 18:31, however, it is God who hears his cries and draws (literally "allures") the enemy away from him.

God Loves the Weak and Controls the War

The authors of 1 and 2 Chronicles are espeically fond of having humbled, weak, and meek Israelites call upon God for help and rescue (e.g. 2 Chron 14:9–15 [vv. 8–14 in the Hebrew]); 2 Chron 12:6; 2 Chron 20:12; 2 Chron 16:8). This theme of God rescuing helpless persecuted people is at the heart of Israel's very founding myth the Exodus, in which Yahweh rescues an enslaved people from oppressive tyrants (see also Deut 7:7–8). (See Kasher, esp. 246–247.) For Millard C. Lind, the exodus theme provides the early paradigm for a positive biblical political ethic. In a sense, Lind attempts to rehabilitate God the Warrior as a liberator who employs miracles, eliminating the need for human beings to wield sword and shield (1980:34, 36, 87–88). Israel has no weaponry, no army, only God to wrest freedom from bondage through the miracles of the plagues, culminating in the parting of the sea and the drowning of the Egyptian pursuers, including Pharaoh himself (Exodus 15:4).

This image of Israel's helplessness and her cries to God also help to shape the Deuteronomic corpus. Deuteronomy pictures God as a loving parent, scooping up his threatened child from those who would harm her. Over and over, in the book of Judges Israel cries to the Lord in distress and he raises up a savior for his people, doomed to frequent subjugation because of their own sinfulness (Judges 2:16–23; 3:9; 3:15; 4:3; 6:7, etc). Battle accounts, moreover, present a theme important also in Chronicles that Israel's force, when she does fight herself, should reveal the power of God.

God may reveal his strength and Israel's weakness by ordering the army to be small in number on purpose (Judges 7:4–7). Before the battle with the Midianites, the leader Gideon is told by God that all the soldiers who drink water directly from a pool by lapping it up are to fight, whereas those who cup the water in their hands and drink are to be set aside. God thus selects his soldiers in an entirely arbitrary or random manner and cuts the potential army to a force of only three hundred men (7:6–8). The enemy is said to be a multitude "lying in the valley, as numerous as locusts," "their camels impossible to count, as numerous as the sand on the sea-shore" (7:12). But with God, Gideon wins as predicted by a divinely sent dream, whose report and interpretation Gideon overhears as a sign before the battle (Judges 7:13–14). In a similar manner, King Amaziah of Judah is told to limit his force to Judahites (2 Chron 25:7–8) and to exclude Ephraimites of whom God does not approve. He listens and succeeds. Similarly, King Asa is informed by the prophet Hanani that his admission of weakness and reliance on God alone had allowed him victory over a massive force of Ethiopians and Libyans (2 Chron 16:8). To rely on an Aramaean alliance, however, guarantees defeat and a constant state of war (2 Chron 16:7–9).

Miracles

The power of God and the helplessness of human fighters is also conveyed by a lengthy biblical tradition of wars presented as miracle accounts (Lind 1980: 34, 36, and throughout). We have already mentioned the victory over Pharaoh, the most formative of biblical wars fought by God for Israel. There are many others, such as the battle with Amalek won through the sympathetic magic of Moses' raised hands (Ex 17:8–13); the battle that succeeds when the walls of Jericho fall down (Josh 6:20); the victory allowed by the sun's standing still for Joshua (Josh 10:12–13); the stretched-out javelin that symbolizes and brings about victory at Ai (Josh 8:18); the mighty voice of God that puts the Philistines into disarray at 1 Sam 7:9–11; the blindness that disables the Aramaean enemy at 2 Kgs 6:18; the God-sent illusion of a huge army that sends the Aramaens into disarray at 2 Kgs 7:5–7; and the rescue of King Hezekiah's Judah from invading Assyrians under Sennacherib when "the angel of the Lord," Exodus-like, comes in the night and kills 185,000 of the enemy in their camp (2 Kgs 19:35–37). Also of interest in the context of victory through divine miracles is 2 Kgs 3:20–25 when again Exodus-like God brings flood and blood upon

Moab to trick them into defeat. But when Israel's victory seems assured the King of Moab offers his first-born son as a sacrifice (presumably to his own god, but the text does not say) and the tide turns in favor of Moab (see chapter 1). The Chronicler altogether omits the intriguing juxtaposition of scenes in 2 Kings 3:20–27, implying that the power of human sacrifice offered in war may counter the power of God-sent, prophetically predicted miracles. The authors of 1 and 2 Chronicles do, however, enrich other biblical war portrayals with miracle accounts such as those described above, including some found in the Deuteronomic History (e.g. the escape from Sennacherib [2 Kgs 19:35–37 = 2 Chron 32:20–23]), embellishing others (compare the brief reference to the war of Abijam in 1 Kgs 15:6 with the account in 2 Chron 13:14–19), and creating new ones such as 2 Chron 20:1–30, a miraculous victory over Moab and Ammon. The miracle accounts combine with images of the people's and leaders' utter helplessness before the foreign enemies to reveal a God who himself runs the war and achieves victory.

In this concept of the God-run, often miraculously achieved victory are the seeds of an ideology of non-participation. First, we provide some brief implicit indications of this ideology and then an extended examination of 2 Chron 20.

At 1 Chron 12:16–18, Benjaminites and Judahites come to David, asking to join his band of warriors. In this account that has no parallel in the Deuteronomic corpus David responds to them, "If in peace you have come to me to help me, you and I will be of one heart but if to betray me to my enemies . . . the God of our ancestors will see and render judgment." On the one hand, David appears to invoke a covenantal-style curse, threatening divine punishment for those who would deceive and betray him. On the other hand, such a curse also places matters of revenge in God's hands.

The threat of God's power is also adequate to guarantee the peace at 2 Chron 17:10–19. "The fear of the Lord was upon all the kingdoms of the lands surrounding Judah and they did not wage war with Jehoshaphat" (17:10.) In a motif reminiscent of the Egyptians' sending out the pesky, plague-bringing Israelites with gifts of gold and silver jewelry and clothing upon request (Ex 12:35–36), the passage goes on to list the gifts of tribute brought to Jehoshaphat by Philistines and Arabs (2 Chron 17:11). The realpolitik of buying peace from the more powerful state thus intertwines with the theme of God's imposing the peace on his own terms. So in Exodus 12:36, "Yahweh gave the people favor in the eyes of the Egyptians and they handed them (the goods) over and they (Israel) plundered Egypt." The passage that best combines themes of helplessness, reliance on God, and divine control of war and peace, approaching the ideology of non-participation in the fighting by Israelites themselves, is 2 Chronicles 20. A "great multitude" is about to attack Judah. The king Jehoshaphat responds not with the bravado of the bardic war tradition nor with some version of the pragmatic ideology of expediency nor with the marginal's address to deception and trickery. The text, meaning to portray him most favorably, says simply "He was scared and gave himself over to seek out the Lord" (2 Chron 20:3). This is for the author the proper response for the leader.

In a dramatic scene, Jehoshaphat delivers an eloquent prayer. The speech framed as a prayer to God by a leader and delivered before a great throng on a special occasion or time of crisis is a favorite genre in late biblical literature [Solomon's speech at the dedication of the Temple (1 Kings 8); Ezra's prayer at Ezra 9:3–15; the confessional prayer at Neh 9:1–37]. In Ezra 9, Nehemiah 9, and 2 Chronicles 20 the leader (Ezra 9:5) or the whole people have been fasting (Neh 9:1; 2 Chron 20:3). Such an act of atonement acknowledges that the enemy can succeed only if Israel has been faithless to God. If she atones for her sins, the enemies' progress may be halted. The act of fasting and the words of the leader's speech emphasize Israel's weaknesses moral and physical, past and current (Ezra 9:5–7, 10; Neh 9:9, 16; 2 Chron 20:7, 11) and recall the ways in which God has saved his people from disaster in the past (2 Chron 20:6–7; Ezra 9:9; Neh 9:6–15, 19–25). The leader petitions God for help or forgiveness (Ezra 9:15) in the present as he saved Israel's ancestors in the past (2 Chron 20:12; Neh 9:31–32). God's capacity for mercy is invoked in a manner both wish-fulfilling for the petitioners and obsequious toward God the Judge (2 Chron 20:9; Ezra 9:8, 15; Neh 9:17–19, 28, 31, 33).

In Ezra 9 and Nehemiah 9, the confessional theme with its emphasis on moral weaknesses is particularly strong. In 2 Chronicles 20, a war text, the emphasis is more on the people's inability to withstand the aggressors who are ready to invade and conquer. God is not only reminded that he drove out the pre-Israelite inhabitants of the land, but also that it was his command not to utterly destroy the people of Ammon, Moab, and Mt. Seir who now threaten (2 Chron 20:10-12). The tradition found also in Deut 2:1-19 that etiologizes the existence and well-being of some of Israel's regional competitors is thus invoked here as a just complaint by Jehoshaphat, requiring God's defense of his people. If God allowed these enemies to live, he must now deal with them (2 Chron 20:12).

The people's utter powerlessness is addressed in Jehoshaphat's speech. "We have no strength before this great multitude that comes against us. And we, we do not know what we will do, but our eyes are on you" (2 Chron 20:12). The image of dependence is further reinforced by the image at v. 13 of "all Judah standing before the Lord with their little ones, their wives, and their children."

The scene is tense, wrapped in pathos. Suddenly God's response comes as the spirit of prophecy descends upon Jahaziel, a member of the priestly clan of Asaph, who is standing in the midst of the crowd. At the heart of the divine message is v. 17. "It is not for you to fight. Station yourselves and stand still and see the victory of the Lord for you. Judah and Jerusalem, do not fear, do not be dismayed. Tomorrow go before them, for the Lord is with you." The advice is not to fight or how to fight or to accept conquest instead of fighting. Victory is promised but not through human hands.

The dramatic scene continues. Jehoshaphat and the people bow down gratefully to God. Early the next morning they gather together; their king encourages them to believe in God's word through his prophets. The priestly singers lead forth the troops, who are not to fight, with a song of thanksgiving. As they sing, the enemy invaders miraculously fall upon one another until they are destroyed. The scene that greets the Judeans is one of corpses and booty, so much booty that it takes three days to gather it up (2 Chron 20:25). As in the Exodus, without raising a hand, they despoil their enemies of their goods and their lives.

The intervention by a deity to save his people by creating a chaos of slaughter in the enemy camp or by eliminating them more directly through an angel of death (as in 2 Chron 32:21 = 2 Kgs 19:35) is not unique to Israelite literature (Doran:48). The way in which the author of 2 Chronicles 20 makes this topos his own is, however, significant for our study of the ideologies of war. It is the culmination, or one logical extension of a lengthy biblical tradition presenting God as the rescuer of the people Israel. If all is in God's hands, the victories and the defeats, why should mere humans fight? If the granting of life and the decreeing of death are divine prerogatives, why should humans make decisions in war that govern life and death? This ideology stands in stark contrast to the ideology of expedience. As Elisha responds at 2 Kgs 6:22 to the question about captured invaders, "Father, should I kill them?" (6:21), "Do not kill them! Are these people whom *you* took captive with *your* sword and *your* bow that you want to kill?" However, whereas the passage in 2 Kings 6 beneficently has the prisoners fed, clothed, and returned to their master, 1 Chronicles 20 revels in the enemies' death and despoilment.

The inchoate, nascent ideology of non-participation is thus not an ideology of non-violence. An appropriator might put together passages such as 2 Chronicles 20, 2 Chron 28:9–11, and 2 Kgs 6:22–23 and begin to construct a more non-violent ideology of confrontation, but the ideology of war as it emerges in 2 Chronicles 20 leaves fully intact the troubling image of Yahweh the destroyer, Yahweh the God who plays favorites and protects only his own. As in the ideology of the ban as God's justice, one might justify the killing as deserved punishment—after all it is the Moabites and Ammonites who are the aggressors—or one might fall back as must the author of Job upon the mystery of God's ways. That is, God might have eliminated the threat of the Moabites and their allies in less violent miraculous ways (as in 2 Kings 6) but does not for reasons we cannot comprehend. Such a line of questions, however, begins to move beyond the primary concern of this study, the ideologies of war of the ancient Israelites.

While the author of 2 Chronicles 20 can imagine divinely commanded non-participation by Israelites in war, he does not imagine elimination of the killing and the violence. Indeed the case might be made that in portraying God as doing all the killing, he wipes his hands of human responsibility for the slaughter and need do less ideologically to justify or rationalize his pleasure in the image of profiting from the enemies' violent deaths. As for the authors and audiences of Esther, permission has been granted from a higher authority that permits the killing, and in this case the higher authority does the killing himself. And yet if one extends the implicit wa ideology of 2 Chronicles to mean that God will always do the fighting then one has taken a step towards containment of war-making.

Like the ideology of the ban as God's justice, the ideology of non-participation belongs not to the powerful able to impose their will but to the disenfranchised who identify with the powerless Judeans, their wives and children, who stand trembling in fearful anticipation of their destruction by invading enemies. One response to such powerlessness is to imagine taking up arms in a righteous cause and with God's help utterly eliminating the evil and unjust enemy in open combat (i.e. the ideology of the ban as God's justice), another is to imagine striking at the enemy less completely and more covertly through trickery and deception, employing the tools of the assassin (the ideology of tricksterism). 2 Chronicles 20 and the other miracle war accounts with which it shares a trajectory offer another option to those who lack political, economic, or social power, divine intervention. Only this option does not encourage the waging of war, instead urging its adherents to wait for God. War is safely set on "the sacred shelf" (Gewertz:325–26; Niditch, 1980:173) out of Israrel's reach.

Taken as a whole, the various threads we have explored in 1 and 2 Chronicles—the elimination of certain references to David's cruelty, the genealogical treatment of the conquest that leaves out the ban, the emphasis on Solomon's status as a leader of peace allowed to build God's holy dwelling on earth, the positive value of Israel's helplessness, a helplessness that encourages God to assume the role of rescuer, and the emphasis on victory in war as divinely sent miracle, the most dramatic examples of which command no human to fight at all—reveal a late biblical tradition groping toward peace. The Chroniclers build upon sentiments and images available in earlier biblical tradition but combine them to make a breakthrough toward an ideology of peace.

Conclusions

A Rabbinic tradition relates that God's ministering angels sought to chant in jubilation after the Israelites had crossed the Red Sea. Their song, however, is stayed by God. "The work of my hands has drowned in the sea and shall you chant songs?" God does not "rejoice in the downfall of the wicked" (bMeg 10b; bSan 39b). In the eyes of the Rabbis, the Egyptians deserve their fate, but they too are God's creations, God's children.

When my family arrives at the rhythmic listing of the plagues in the Passover seder and the ceremonial spilling of the wine, a drop for each plague, someone always says, "Remember how Pa used to cry at the plagues?" My grandfather would participate in a sort of ritual wailing for the Egyptians, an action counterpart for the midrashic story about God's staying the angels' song. There were causes in his own life for sadness, and perhaps in the crying he identified with the Egyptians and found release, reaching out beyond the community of Israel to the community of humankind, bonded by Job-like experiences and the rocky relationships all of us share with the powerful forces of authority, familial, political, and divine.

The midrash about the angels' song is a significant extension of the ideology of non-participation. The biblical foundation myth of the Exodus presenting an implicit war ideology in which human beings do not fight their enemies, now enriched by a post-biblical tradition, reflects and enjoins pity for the enemies' suffering in defeat. The joy experienced in the liberation of one's own people, a victory made possible by God's war against an oppressive tyrant, is tempered by sorrow for the enemy.

It would be comforting and uplifting to end our work by suggesting that this is the direction taken uniformly by post-biblical Judaism. In similar fashion, a Christian scholar might be happy to conclude by offering readers an ideology of peace and non-violence espoused by all Christians inspired by reflections upon the Jesus event, the founding myth of Judaism's sister religion.

Such descriptions of post-biblical war ideologies in either tradition would, of course, be as facile and inaccurate as any suggestion that there ever was one ancient Israelite war ideology. People and cultures are more complex than that.

The Passover tradition revealed in my grandfather's tears is held in tension with other traditions concerning the treatment of Egyptian enemies, enshrined in the Haggadah, the text for the Passover seder. Commentaries such as that of Rabbi Akiva suggest, for example, in a wish-fulfilling way that each plague was really five plagues. The song Dayenu, meaning "It would be enough for us," usually performed in a children's singsong melody lists all of God's "good deeds" for Israel. The song includes lines such as "If he had killed their first-born and had not given us their weatlh, it would be enough for us!" The serious lyrics and the lighthearted melody lend a macabre quality to exultation in the enemy's defeat. Other Rabbinic commentaries on Exodus take ghoulish pleasure in the suffering of the Egyptians in the plagues and at the Red Sea. One tradition suggests, for example, that the frogs castrated the Egyptians (Exodus Rabbah 9:10). All of us clearly have the capacity both to love and to hate our enemies.

The war traditions of the Hebrew Scriptures genuinely grapple with issues of compassion and enmity. The many war texts we have sorted and explored on some basic level reveal human beings' attempts to make sense of war and of killing in war. In the process, the biblical writers define themselves as individuals and as members of groups, variously delineated, as people in an ongoing relationship with a preeminently powerful and often inscrutable deity, variously understood, and as opponents to many other individuals and groups who hold competing claims and values. We have uncovered several trajectories.

The ban as sacrifice is an ideology of war in which the enemy is to be utterly destroyed as an offering to the deity who has made victory possible. Implicit in this ideology is a view of God who appreciates human sacrifice and a curious respect for human life. Human beings are the most desirable and valuable offerings and are the portion of God. The Israelites are often portrayed keeping animal and inanimate spoil. Also implicit in the ban as sacrifice is a sense of inevitability that allows the killers to eschew responsibility for the kill. God demands all the humans as an offering. No decision to spare this person and kill that one need be made. The enemy is never kin, an Israelite, nor however, is he a monster. He is a human, a mirror of the self whose destruction is a promised sacrifice exchanged for victory. This ideology of war is probably as ancient as Israel itself or more accurately as ancient as the precursors of that group that would be called Israel, but is a view of war, the deity, and the enemy's death that is preserved in some form throughout Israelite history.

The ideology of the ban as God's justice reflects an attempt to make sense of Israelite banning traditions in terms of right and wrong, good and bad, a Deuteronomic ethic of deserved blessing and curse. Enemies are totally annihilated because they are sinners, condemned under the rules of God's justice. Killing in war thus might be rationalized and guilt assuaged. The Israelites are to be regarded as God's instrument of justice and the enemy is a less-than-human monster who must be eradicated. The enemy is unclean and his uncleanness may contaminate non-human booty that belonged to him, especially when the enemy is a fellow Israelite or a group of fellow Israelites, for this ban can be directed against those perceived as the enemy within.

The concept of the ban as God's justice seems especially appropriate for the seventh-century BCE reformers who preserved much of the biblical conquest and other warring traditions, but belongs also to their precursors and offspring in the tradition. This ideology is not reliant upon the notion of a god who appreciates human offerings, an idea anathema to these reformers, but is entirely relevant to the Deuteronomic concept of Israel as a "pristine entity" that had become soiled by idolatrous enemies within and without the people. A society under siege, Israel must be purified and cleansed of contaminating influences.

The priestly ideology of war in Numbers 31 reveals similarities to the ban as God's justice. The enemy is regarded as deserving of God's vengeance and is almost annihilated, but virgin girls are spared. This glitch in a war ideology allowing for massive destruction stems from the post-monarchic, priestly emphasis on clean and unclean that frames the ideology as a whole. Women children who have not lain with a man are clean slates in terms of their identity, unmarked by the enemy and, after a period of purification, can be absorbed into the people Israel. So too booty can be kept after purification and distributed for the use of God, his priests, and the people. The emphasis on the need for purification is stronger in Numbers 31 than in the Deuteronomic ban as God's justice. The uncleanness, however, is not only a matter of contagion from the idolatrous enemy. The very act of killing in war renders the Israelite soldier unclean. He too must be purified before resuming his life as a whole member of the people Israel. In this way, a late-biblical ideology of war acknowledges the humanity of the enemy whose death tears the orderly fabric of the Israelite universe even while insisting upon the necessity of eliminating the impure "Other." This ideology thus underlines some of the deep paradoxes implicit in biblical ethics of violence.

The bardic tradition, so called because of the beautiful traditional-style narration in which much of the material is preserved, presents a view of war that glorifies warriors, their courage, daring, leadership, and skill. Respect is apparent between enemies whose confrontations sometimes take the form of a duel and involve a stylized form of war behavior, taunting. The image of war as a men's game or sport is strong, as is the emphasis on a code of fair play in the game that is war. Men, for example, should fight their equals in experience and skill. Spoil in goods and women is sought after and enjoyed but sometimes leads to conflict among allies. This all too beautified picture of war nevertheless lays a foundation for an Israelite *jus in bello*. The bardic tradition preserves an aristocratic, prettified view of war that may well have its origins in the royal courts of Judah.

The ideology of tricksterism is a war ethic of the underdog who must use deception or trickery to improve his lot. Akin to guerilla warfare, the ideology of the trickster does not admit of guilt concerning the enemy's death and allows for no code in the fighting, though the cause is always just from the perspective of the tricksters. Tricksterism, an avenue available to those out of power, is an ideology probably as old as the people Israel, available to Israelites throughout their difficult history of subjugation.

The ideology of expediency suggests that once there is war, anything can be done to achieve objectives. Once the war is won, anything can be done to subjugate the defeated enemy. In contrast to tricksterism, this is an ideology of the powerful, able to employ brutality to achieve military goals, defensive or offensive. The war is sometimes argued to be just but oftentimes involves naked aggression and conquest—all undertaken, according to the adherents of this ideology, with God's blessing. The formulaic language typical of the ban is sometimes found, but without a framework of self-justification, be it the need to give God his portion or to kill sinners. This ideology treats war as business as usual, practiced by Israelite rulers and their ancient Near Eastern counterparts.

The ideology of non-participation is rooted in biblical traditions that describe God's capacity to save Israel through the performance of miracles. These traditions are reinforced by prophetic injunctions not to rely on mere humans and their governments for salvation. The ideology of non-participation suggests that the people need not fight wars. God, in fact, loves a helpless, faithful people best. As he heard the cries of the powerless Hebrew slaves in Egypt and redeemed them, so he will save his people again. The neatest portrayal of this ideology is found in the late biblical 2 Chronicles 20. Non-participation offers the powerless an alternative to other ethics of war.

The several war ideologies explored in our study are neither self-contained nor related to one another in simple chronological sequences in the social, religious, and intellectual history of Israel. It has been customary for scholars to suggest that the ban (treated usually as one phenomenon) is an early ideology or actual form of warfare in ancient Israel that was replaced by more pragmatic war beliefs and behaviors under the monarchy or that the ban, acknowledged by some as early, by others as late, had its heyday as an ideology only during the Josianic reform or in the social tensions of the exile.

In fact, the history of attitudes to war in ancient Israel is a complex one involving multiplicity, overlap, and self-contradiction. There is more than one variety of ban ideology, and various war ideologies coexist during any one period in the history of Israel. The priestly ideology of war has much in common with the ideology of the ban as God's justice while the violent pragmatism of the ideology of expediency is reflected also in the ideology of tricksterism. Those whose courts produced the ennobling bardic tradition may well have practiced the brutal ideology of expediency. Those who imagine God fighting and not humans thereby planting seeds for pacifists later in the western tradition nevertheless express desires to utterly destroy certain of their own kinsmen.

All of the attitudes to war we have uncovered in the Hebrew Scriptures are as old as human culture itself and as complex as human thought, linking our earliest ancestors with ourselves and our neighbors' cultures with our own. This study has explored the ways in which seven ideologies of war emerge in the biblical tradition of ancient Israel, examining why and how each one may have functioned among Israelites of particular situations and settings. We have asked not only how the ideologies of war reflect Israelite cultures but also how various war-views have affected and molded Israelite self-understanding. These currents in and influences upon the course of Israelite social and intellectual history do not lose their force with the close of the biblical period but continue to inform attitudes to war and peace and to define the conflict within each of us between compassion and enmity.

REFERENCES

Abel, F.M. 1950. "L'anathème de Jericho et la maison de Rahab." *RB* 57:321–30.

Aho, James A. 1981. *Religious Mythology and the Art of War. Comparative Religious Symbolisms of Military Violence.* Westport, CT: Greenwood Press.

Albright, William Foxwell. 1957. *From the Stone Age to Christianity.* Garden City, NY: Doubleday.

Alt, Albrecht. 1959. *Kleine Schriften zur Geschichte des Volkes Israel.* Band I. München: C.H. Beck'sche Verlagsbuchhandlung.

Alter, Robert. 1981. *The Art of Biblical Narrative.* New York: Basic Books.

———. 1985. *The Art of Biblical Poetry.* New York: Basic Books.

Anderson, Bernard W. 1954. *Esther.* IB3.

———. 1957. *Understanding the Old Testament.* Englewood Cliffs, NJ: Prentice Hall.

Anderson, Gary A. 1954. *Sacrifices and Offerings in Ancient Israel. Studies in their Social and Political Importance. HSM* 41. Atlanta: Scholars.

Bainton, Roland H. 1960. *Christian Attitudes Toward War and Peace.* Nashville: Abingdon.

Barton, John. 1978. "Understanding Old Testament Ethics." *JSOT* 9:44–64.

Barucq, A. 1959. *Judith, Esther.* La Sainte Bible. Paris: Editions du Cerf.

Birch, Bruce C. and Larry L. Rasmussen. 1976. *Bible and Ethics in the Christian Life.* Minneapolis, MN: Augsburg.

Bohannan, Paul, ed. 1967. *Law and Warfare: Studies in the Anthropology of Conflict.* Garden City, NY: Natural History Press.

Boling, Robert G. 1975. *Judges. Introduction, Translation and Commentary.* Anchor Bible. Garden City, NY: Doubleday.

———. 1982. *Joshua: A New Translation with Notes and Commentary.* Anchor Bible. Garden City, NY: Doubleday.

Bramson, Leon and George W. Goethals, eds. 1968. *War. Studies from Psychology, Sociology, Anthropology.* New York: Basic.

Brekelmans, C.H.W. 1959a. *La ḥērem in het Oude Testament.* Nijmegen: Centrale drukkerij.

———. 1959b. "Le ḥerem chez les prophètes du royaume du Nord et dans le Deutéronome." *Sacra pagina.* I. *Bibliotheca ephemeridum theologicarum lovansienum* 12/13:377-83.

Bright, John. 1981. *A History of Israel.* Third Edition. Philadelphia: Westminster.

Bruce, W.S. 1909. *The Ethics of the Old Testament.* Edinburgh: T and T, Clark.

Budd, Philip J. 1984. *Numbers. Word Biblical Commentary.* Waco, TX: Word Books.

Burkert, Walter. 1983. *Homo Necans. The Anthropology of Ancient Greek Sacrificial Ritual and Myth.* Berkeley: University of California.

———. 1987. "The Problem of Ritual Killing." In Robert G. Hammerton-Kelly, ed. *Violent Origins.* 149-76.

Burridge, Kenelm. 1969. *New Heaven New Earth: A Study of Millenarian Activities.* New York: Schocken.

Camp, Claudia V. 1985. *Wisdom and the Feminine in the Book of Proverbs.* Sheffield: *JSOT.*

Camp, Claudia V. and Carole R. Fontaine. 1990. "The Words of the Wise and their Riddles." In Susan Niditch, ed. *Text and Tradition: The Hebrew Bible and Folklore.* Atlanta: Scholars. 127-51.

Carmody, John, Denise Lardner Carmody, and Robert L. Cohn. 1988. *Exploring the Hebrew Bible.* Englewood Cliffs, NJ: Prentice Hall.

Carpenter, C.R. 1967. "The Contribution of Primate Studies to the Understanding of War." In Morton Fried, Marvin Harris, and Robert Murphy, eds. *War: The Anthropology of Armed Conflict and Aggression.* 49-58.

Chagnon, Napoleon. 1967. "Yanomamö Social Organization and Warfare." In Morton Fried, Marvin Harris, and Robert Murphy, eds. *War: The Anthropology of Armed Conflict and Aggression.* 109-58.

———. 1977. *Yanomamö. The Fierce People.* New York: Holt, Rinehart and Winston.

Childs, Brevard S. 1970. *Biblical Theology in Crisis.* Philadelphia: Westminster.

———. 1979. *Introduction to the Old Testament As Scripture.* Philadelphia: Fortress.

Christensen, Duane L. 1975. *The Transformation of the War Oracle in Old Testament Prophecy.* Missoula: Scholars.

Cohen, Ronald. 1984. "Warfare and State Formation: Wars Make States and States Make War." In Brian Ferguson, ed. *Warfare, Culture, and Environment.* 329–358.

Cohn, Norman. 1961. *The Pursuit of Millennium.* Harper: New York.

Coogan, Michael David. 1978. *Stories From Ancient Canaan.* Philadelphia: Westminster.

Coote, Robert B. and Keith W. Whitelam. 1987. *The Emergence of Early Israel in Historical Perspective.* Sheffield: Almond.

Coote, Robert and David Robert Ord. 1989. *The Bible's First History.* Philadelphia: Fortress.

Craigie, Peter C. 1978. *The Problem of War in the Old Testament.* Grand Rapids, MI: Eerdmans.

Crenshaw, James L. 1978. *Samson: A Secret Betrayed, a Vow Ignored.* Atlanta: John Knox.

———. 1985. "Education in Ancient Israel." *JBL* 104:601–15.

Crenshaw, James L. and John J. Willis, eds. 1974. *Essays in Old Testament Ethics.* J. Philip Hyatt, In Memoriam. New York: KTAV.

Cross, Frank Moore. 1975. "A Reconstruction of the Judean Restoration." *Interpretation* 29:187–203.

Daly, Martin and Margo Wilson. 1988. *Homicide.* New York: Aldine De Gruyter.

Daube, David. 1965. *Collaboration with Tyranny in Rabbinic Law.* The Riddell Memorial Lectures, 1965. London: Oxford University Press.

Davie, Maurice R. 1929. *The Evolution of War: A Study of its Role in Early Societies.* New Haven: Yale University.

Day, John. 1989. *Molech: A God of Human Sacrifice in Old Testament.* University of Cambridge Oriental Publications No. 41. Cambridge, England: Cambridge University.

Day, Peggy L. 1989a. "From the Child Is Born The Woman: The Story of Jephthah's Daughter." In Peggy L. Day, ed. *Gender and Difference in Ancient Israel.* Minneapolis: Fortress. 58–74.

———. 1989b, ed. *Gender and Difference in Ancient Israel.* Minneapolis: Fortress.

Dearman, Andrew, ed. 1989. *Studies in the Mesha Inscription and Moab.* Atlanta: Scholars Press.

de Geus, C.H.J. 1976. *The Tribes of Israel. An Investigation into Some of the Presuppositions of Martin Noth's Amphictyony Hypothesis.* Studia Semitica Neerlandica 18. Assen.

de Vaulx, J. 1972. *Les Nombres. Sources Bibliques.* Paris: J. Gabalda et Cie.

de Vaux, Roland. 1961a. "Review of C.H.W. Brekelmans, *De ḥerem.*" *RB* 68:294–95.

———. 1961b. *Ancient Israel: Its Life and Institutions.* New York: McGraw Hill.

———. 1966. "Single Combat in the Old Testament." In Roland de Vaux, ed. *The Bible and the Ancient Near East.* Garden City, NY: Doubleday. 122–135.

Doran, Robert. 1982. *Temple Propaganda: The Purpose and Character of 2 Maccabees.* CBQMS 12; Washington, D.C.: CBA.

Douglas, Mary. 1966. *Purity and Danger. An Analysis of Concepts of Pollution and Taboo.* New York: Praeger.

Duff, Archibald. 1902. *The Theology and Ethics of the Hebrews.* New York: Charles Scribner's Sons.

Eibl-Eibesfeldt, Irenäus. 1979. *The Biology of Peace and War: Men, Animals and Aggression.* New York: Viking.

Eichrodt, Walther. 1961. *Theology of the Old Testament.* Philadelphia: Westminster.

Eissfeldt, O. 1951. "Ein gescheiterer Versuch der Weidervereinigung Israels (2 Sam 2:12–31)." *La Nouvelle Clio* 3:110–27.

———. 1952. "Noch einmal: Ein gescheiterer Versuch der Weidervereinigung Israels." *La Nouvelle Clio* 4:55–59.

Eliade, Mircea. 1971. *The Myth of the Eternal Return or, Cosmos and History.* Bollingen Series XLVI. Princeton, N.J.: Princeton University.

Emerton, J.A. 1971b. "The Riddle of Genesis XIV." *VT* 21:403–39.

Evans-Pritchard, E.E. 1940. *The Nuer.* Oxford: Clarendon.

Ferguson, Brian, ed. 1984. *Warfare, Culture, and Environment.* Orlando: Academic Press.

Fishbane, Michael. 1985. *Biblical Interpretation in Ancient Israel.* Oxford/New York: Oxford University Press.

Fohrer, Georg. 1968. *Introduction to the Old Testament.* Nashville: Abingdon.

———. 1972. *History of Israelite Religion.* Nashville: Abingdon.

Fortes, Meyer. 1940. "The Political System of the Tallesi of the Northern Territories of the Gold Coast." In M. Fortes and E.E. Evans-Pritchard, eds. *African Political Systems.* London: Oxford University Press. 239–71.

Fortes, M. and E.E. Evans-Pritchard, eds. *African Political Systems.* London: Oxford University Press.

———. 1940. "Introduction." In *African Political Systems.* London: Oxford University Press. 1–23.

Fowler, Mervin D. 1987. "The Meaning of *lipnê* YHWH in the Old Testament." *ZAW* 99:384–90.

Freedman, D.N. and D.F. Graf, eds. 1983. *Palestine in Transition: The Emergence of Ancient Israel.* Sheffield: Almond.

Frick, Frank S. 1979. "Religion and Sociopolitical Structure in Early Israel: An Ethno-Archaeological Approach." In *SBL* Seminar Papers. 233–53.

———. 1985. *The Formation of the State in Ancient Israel.* Decatur: Almond.

Fried, Morton, Marvin Harris, and Robert Murphy, eds. 1967. *War: The Anthropology of Armed Conflict and Aggression.* Garden City, NY: Natural History Press.

Friedman, Richard E. 1987. *Who Wrote the Bible?* Englewood Cliffs, NJ: Prentice Hall.

Friedmann, Meir. 1870. *Mekilta.* Vienna.

Gabriel, Ingeborg. 1990. *Friede über Israel. Eine Untersuchung zur Frie denstheologie in Chronik I 10–II 36.* Klosterneuberg: Verlag Österreichisches Katholisches Bibelwerk.

Gewertz, Deborah. 1980. "Of Symbolic Anchors and Sago Soup: The Rhetoric of Exchange Among the Chambri of Papua New Guinea." *Journal of the Polynesian Society* 89:309–28.

Girard, René. 1977. *Violence and the Sacred.* Trans. Patrick Gregory. Baltimore: Johns Hopkins.

———. 1987. "Generative Scapegoating." In Robert G. Hammerton-Kelly, ed. *Violent Origins.* 73–105.

Gluckman, Max. 1973. *Custom and Conflict in Africa.* New York: Harper and Row.

Goldin, Judah. 1967. "Introduction" to *The Last Trial* by Shalom Spiegel. New York: Schocken.

Good, Robert M. 1985. "The Just War in Ancient Israel." *JBL* 104:385–400.

Gottwald, Norman. 1964. "'Holy War' in Deuteronomy: Analysis and Critique." *Review and Expositor* 61:297–310.

———. 1979. *The Tribes of Yahweh: A Sociology for the Religion of Liberated Israel 1250–1050 BCE.* Maryknoll, NY: Orbis Books.

Graham, M. Patrick. 1989. "The Discovery and Reconstruction of the Mesha Inscription." In Andrew Dearman, ed. *Studies in the Mesha Inscription and Moab.* 41–92.

Gray, George Buchanan. 1903. *A Critical and Exegetical Commentary on Numbers.* New York: Charles Scribner's Sons.

Green, Alberto Ravinell Whitney. 1975. *The Role of Human Sacrifice in the Ancient Near East.* ASOR Diss. Ser. 1. Missoula, MT: Scholars.

Halpern, Baruch. 1988a. *The First Historians. The Hebrew Bible and History*. San Francisco: Harper and Row.

———. 1988b. "The Assassination of Eglon—the First Locked-Room Murder Mystery." *BR* 6:32–41; 44.

Hammerton-Kelly, Robert G., ed. 1987. *Violent Origins. Walter Burkert, René Girard, and Jonathan Z. Smith on Ritual Killing and Cultural Formation*. Stanford, CA: Stanford University.

Hanson, Paul D. 1987. "War, Peace, and Justice in Early Israel." *BR* 3:32–45.

Harris, Marvin. 1974. *Cows, Pigs, Wars and Witches*. New York: Random House.

———. 1977. *Cannibals and Kings. The Origins of Cultures*. New York: Random House.

———. 1979. *Cultural Materialism. The Struggle for a Science of Culture*. New York: Random House.

Harris, William V. 1989. *Ancient Literacy*. Cambridge, MA: Harvard University.

Heidel, Alexander. 1951. *The Babylonian Genesis*. Chicago/London: University of Chicago.

Heider, George C. 1985 *The Cult of Molek. A Reassessment*. Sheffield: JSOT Press.

Hempel, Johannes. 1962. "Ethics in the OT." *IDB*. Vol 2:153–61.

———. 1964. *Das Ethos des alten Testaments*. Berlin: Tøpelmann.

Hendin, Herbert and Ann Pollinger Hass. 1984. *Wounds of War. The Psychological Aftermath of Combat in Vietnam*. New York: Basic.

Hobbs, T.R. 1989. *A Time For War. A Study of Warfare in the Old Testament*. Wilmington, Delaware: Michael Glazier, Inc.

Holloway, Ralph L. Jr. 1967. "Human Aggression: The Need for a Species-Specific Framework." In Morton Fried, Marvin Harris, and Robert Murphy, eds. *War: The Anthropology of Armed Conflict and Aggression*. 29–48.

Holmes, Arthur F., ed. 1975. *War and Christian Ethics*. Grand Rapids, MI: Eerdmans.

Jackson, Kent P. 1989. "The Language of the Mesha Inscription." In Andrew Dearman, ed. *Studies in the Mesha Inscription and Moab*. 96–130.

Jackson, Kent P. and J. Andrew Dearman. 1989. "The Text of the Mesha Inscription." In Andrew Dearman, ed. *Studies in the Mesha Inscription and Moab*. 93–95.

Jacobs, Ruth Harriet. 1975. "Sociological Perspectives on the Etiology War." In M.A. Nettleship, R. Dalegivens, and Anderson Nettleship, eds. *War, Its Causes and Correlates*. 29–39.

References   163

Japhet, Sara. 1989. *The Ideology of the Book of Chronicles and Its Place in Biblical Thought.* Frankfurt am Main: Peter Lang.

Johnson, James Turner. 1975. *Ideology, Reason, and the Limitation of War.* Princeton, NJ: Princeton University.

———. 1991. "Historical Roots and Sources of the Just War Tradition in Western Culture." In John Kelsay and James Turner Johnson, eds. *Just War and Jihad.* 3–30.

Johnson, James Turner and John Kelsay. 1990. *Cross, Crescent, and Sword. The Justification and Limitation of War in Western and Islamic Tradition.* New York: Greenwood.

Jones, G. H. 1975. "'Holy War' or 'Yahweh War'." *VT* 25:642–58.

Junker, Herbert. 1947. "Der alttestamentliche Bann gegen heidnische Völker als moraltheologisches und offenbarungs-geschichtliches Problem." In *Trierer theologische Zeitschrift* 56:74–89.

Kaiser, Otto. 1976. "Den Erstgebornen deiner Sohne sollst du mir geben. Erwagungen zum Kinderopfer im alten Testament." In *Denkender Glaube. Festschrift Carl Heinz Ratshow.* Berlin: de Gruyter. 24–48.

Kaiser, Walter C. 1975. *Introduction to the Old Testament. A Presentation of its Results and Problems.* Minneapolis, MN: Augsburg.

———. 1983. *Toward Old Testament Ethics.* Grand Rapids, MI: Zondervan.

Kampen, John. 1988. *The Hasideans and the Origin of Pharisaism. A Study in 1 and 2 Maccabees.* Atlanta: Scholars.

Kang, Sa-Moon. 1989. *Divine War in the Old Testament and in the Ancient Near East.* Berlin/New York: de Gruyter.

Karsten, Rafael. 1923. "Blood Revenge and War Among the Jibaro Indians of Eastern Ecuador." In Paul Bohannan, ed. *Law and Warfare.* 303–25.

Kasher, R. 1985/86. "The Salvation of Jehoshaphat—Its Dimensions, Parallels, Significance." *Bet Mikra* 31:242–51 (Hebrew).

Kelsay, John and James Turner Johnson, eds. 1991. *Just War and Jihad: Historical and Theoretical Perspectives on War and Peace in Western and Islamic Traditions.* New York/Westport, CT: Greenwood.

Knight, Douglas A. 1982. "Old Testament Ethics." *Christian Century.* 99/2:55–59.

La Barbera, Robert. 1984. "The Man of War and the Man of God: Social Satire in 2 Kings 6:8–7:20." *CBQ* 46:637–51.

Lasine, Stuart. 1984. "Guest and Host in Judges 19: Lot's Hospitality in an Inverted World." *JSOT* 29:37–59.

Lasor, William S., David A. Hubbard, and Frederic W. Bush. 1982. *Old Testament Survey. The Message, Form, and Background of the Old Testament.* Grand Rapid, MI: Eerdmans.

Lauterbach, Jacob Z. 1976. *Mekilta De-Rabbi Ishmael*. 3 Vols. Philadelphia: Jewish Publication Society.

Lemche, Niels Peter. 1985. *Early Israel. Anthropological and Historical Studies on the Israelite Society Before the Monarchy*. Leiden: Brill.

———. 1988. *Ancient Israel: A New History of Israelite Society*. Sheffield: JSOT Press.

Lesser, Alexander. 1967. "War and the State." In Morton Fried, Marvin Harris, and Robert Murphy, eds. *War: The Anthropology of Armed Conflict and Aggression*. 92–96.

Levine, Mordecai. 1979. "The Polemic Against Rape in the Song of Deborah." *Beth Mikra* 25:83–84 (Hebrew).

Lind, Millard C. 1980. *Yahweh Is a Warrior: The Theology of Warfare in Ancient Israel*. Scottsdale, PA: Herald Press.

Little, David. 1989. "Religion: Source of Conflict, Source of Peace." Unpublished essay.

———. 1991. "Holy War Appeals and Western Christianity: A Reconsideration of Bainton's Approach. In John Kelsay and James Turner Johnson, eds. *Just War and Jihad: Historical and Theoretical Perspectives on War and Peace in Western and Islamic Traditions*.

Luria, B.Z. 1986/87. "Oded—A Prophet of God." *Dor le-dor* 15:256–59.

Maccoby, Hyam. 1982. *The Sacred Executioner. Human Sacrifice and the Legacy of Guilt*. New York: Thames and Hudson.

McCarter, P. Kyle Jr. 1980. *I Samuel*. Anchor Bible. Garden City, NY: Doubleday.

———. 1984. *II Samuel*. Anchor Bible. Garden City, NY: Doubleday.

McKenzie, Steven L. 1985. *The Chronicler's Use of the Deuteronomistic History*. HSM 33. Atlanta: Scholars.

———. 1991. *The Trouble With Kings. The Composition of the Deuteronomistic History*. Supp. to *VT* 42. Leiden: Brill.

Malamat, Abraham. 1966. "The Ban in Mari and in the Bible." In *Biblical Essays* (proceedings of the 9th Meeting of "Die Ou-Testementiese Werkgemeenskap in Suid-Africa)." Stellenbosch: 40–49.

Malinowski, Bronislaw. 1941. "An Anthropological Analysis of War." In Leon Bramson and George W. Goethals, eds. *War. Studies from Psychology, Sociology, Anthropology*. New York: Basic. 245–68.

Marett, R.R. 1933. *Sacraments of Simple Folk*. Oxford: Clarendon.

Mather, Cotton. 1689. *Souldiers Counselled and Comforted, a Discourse Delivered Unto Some Part of the Forces Engaged in the Just War of New England Against the Northern and Eastern Indians*. September 1, 1689. Boston.

Mattingly, Gerald L. 1989. "Moabite Religion." In Andrew Dearman, ed. *Studies in the Mesha Inscription and Moab*. 211–38.

Mays, James Luther. 1967. *Micah. A Commentary.* Philadelphia: Westminster.

———. 1969. *Amos. A Commentary.* Philadelphia: Westminster.

Mead, George Herbert. 1929. "National Mindedness and International Mindedness." *International Journal of Ethics* 39:385–407.

Mead, Margaret. 1940. "Warfare is Only an Invention—Not a Biological Necessity." In Leon Bramson and George W. Goethals, eds. *War.* 269–74.

Mendenhall, George E. 1973. *The Tenth Generation. The Origin of the Biblical Tradition.* Baltimore: Johns Hopkins.

Meyers, Carol. 1988. *Discovering Eve. Ancient Israelite Women in Context.* New York/Oxford: Oxford University.

Middleton, John. 1963. "Witchcraft and Sorcery in Lugbara." In John Middleton and E.M. Winter, eds. *Witchraft and Sorcery.* 257–75.

Middleton, John and E.H. Winter, eds. 1963. "Introduction." In John Middleton and E.M. Winter, eds. *Witchraft and Sorcery in East Africa.* London: Routledge and Kegan Paul. 1–26.

Milgrom, Jacob. 1978. "Studies in the Temple Scroll." *JBL* 97:501–23.

———. 1981. "The Paradox of the Red Cow (Num XIX)." *VT* 31:62–72.

———. 1990. *Numbers.* Philadelphia: Jewish Publication Society.

Miller, J. Maxwell and John H. Hayes. 1986. *A History of Ancient Israel and Judah.* Philadelphia: Westminster.

Miller, Patrick D. Jr. 1970. "Animal Names as Designations in Ugaritic Hebrew." In *Ugarit-Forschungen* 2. Neukirchen-Vluyn: Butzon and Bercker Kevelear. 177–86.

———. 1975. *The Divine Warrior in Early Israel.* Harvard Semitic Monographs 5. Cambridge, MA: Harvard University.

Mitchell, Hinckley G. 1912. *The Ethics of the Old Testament.* Chicago: University of Chicago.

Mosca, Paul G. 1975. "Child Sacrifice in Canaanite and Israelite Religion: A Study of *mulk* and *mlk*." Unpublished Ph.D. Diss. Harvard University.

Nel, Philip. 1985. "The Riddle of Samson." *Biblica.* 66:534–45.

Nettleship, M.A. 1975. "Definitions." In M.A. Nettleship, R. Dalegivens, and Anderson Nettleship, eds. *War, Its Causes and Correlates.* 73–90.

Nettleship, M.A., R. Dalegivens, and Anderson Nettleship, eds. 1975. *War, Its Causes and Correlates.* The Hague/Paris: Mouton.

Niditch, Susan. 1980. "The Visionary." In George W.E. Nickelsburg and John J. Collins, eds. *Ideal Figures in Ancient Judaism.* Chico, CA: Scholars. 153–79.

———. 1982. "The 'Sodomite' Theme in Judges 19–20: Family, Community, and Social Disintegration." *CBQ* 44:365–78.

——. 1987. *Underdogs and Tricksters: A Prelude to Folklore*. San Francisco: Harper and Row.

——. 1989. "Eroticism and Death in the Tale of Jael." In Peggy L. Day, ed. *Gender and Difference*. 43-57.

——. 1990. "Samson as Culture Hero, Trickster, and Bandit: The Empowerment of the Weak." *CBQ* 52:608-24.

Niditch, Susan, ed. 1990. *Text and Tradition: The Hebrew Bible and Folklore*. Atlanta: Scholars.

Noth, Martin. 1966. *The Old Testament World*. London: Adam and Charles Black.

——. 1968. *Numbers. A Commentary*. Philadelphia: Westminster.

Noy, Dov. 1963. "Riddles in the Wedding Meal." *Mahanayim* 83:64-72.

O'Brien, Mark A. 1989. *The Deuteronomistic History Hypothesis: A Reassessment*. Göttingen: Vandenhoeck and Ruprecht.

Oden, Robert. 1987. *The Bible Without Theology. The Theological Tradition and Alternatives to It*. San Francisco: Harper and Row.

Ollenburger, Ben C. 1991. "Gerhard von Rad's Theory of Holy War." In Gerhard von Rad, *Holy War in Ancient Israel*. 1-33.

Olson, Dennis T. 1985. *The Death of the Old and the Birth of the New. The Framework of the Book of Numbers and the Pentateuch*. Brown Judaic Studies 71. Chico, CA: Scholars.

Olyan, Saul. 1984. "*Hāšālôm*: Some Literary Considerations of 2 Kings 9." *CBQ* 46:652-668.

Paul, Shalom M. 1991. *Amos. A Commentary on the Book of Amos*. Minneapolis: Fortress.

Pedersen, Johannes. 1926/1940. *Israel. Its Life and Culture*. Vols. 1-2; 3-4. London: Oxford University Press.

Polley, Max E. 1989. *Amos and the Davidic Empire. A Socio-Historical Approach*. Oxford/New York: Oxford University.

Pope, Marvin. 1977. *Song of Songs*. Anchor Bible 7c. Garden City, NJ: Doubleday.

Radcliffe-Brown, A.R. 1940. "Preface." In M. Fortes and E.E. Evans-Pritchard, eds. *African Political Systems*. xiv-xxiii.

Rappaport, Roy A. 1968. *Pigs for the Ancestors. Ritual in the Ecology of a New Guinea People*. New Haven: Yale University.

——. 1979. *Ecology, Meaning, and Religion*. Richmond: North Atlantic Books.

Rendtorff, Rolf. 1986. *The Old Testament. An Introduction*. Philadelphia: Fortress.

Rofé, Alexander. 1985. "The Laws of Warfare in the Book of Deuteronomy: Their Origins, Intent, and Positivity." *JSOT* 22:23-44.

Rogerson, John and Philip Davies. 1989. *The Old Testament World*. Englewood Cliffs, NJ: Prentice Hall.

Rubin, Gayle. 1975. "The Traffic of Women: Notes on the Political Economy of Sex." In Rayna R. Reiter, ed. *An Anthropology of Women*. New York: Monthly Review. 157–210.

Sahlins, Marshall D. 1968. *Tribesman. Foundations of Modern Anthropology*. Englewood Cliffs, NJ: Prentice Hall.

Schmid, H.H. 1972. "Heiliger Krieg und Gottesfrieden im alten Testament." In *Altorientalische Welt in der Alttestamentlichen Theologie*. Zurich: Theologische Verlag. 91–120.

Schneider, Joseph. 1950. "Primitive Warfare: A Methodological Note." In Leon Bramson and George W. Goethals, eds. *War*. 293–91.

Schwally, F. 1901. *Semitische Kriegsaltertuemer.I. Der heilige Krieg im Alten Testament*. Leipzig: Deiterich'sche Verlagsbuchhandlung, Theodor Weicher.

Seabury, Paul and Angelo Codevilla. 1989. *War. Ends and Means*. New York: Basic.

Service, Elman R. 1967. "War and our Contemporary Ancestors." In Morton Fried, Marvin Harris, and Robert Murphy, eds. *War: The Anthropology*. 160–69.

Slotkin, Edgar. 1990. "Response to Professors Fontaine and Camp." In Susan Niditch, ed. *Text and Tradition*. 153–59.

Smend, Rudolph. 1970. *Yahweh War and Tribal Confederation: Reflections upon Israel's Earliest History*. Nashville, Abingdon. (Trans. from second German edition of 1966.)

Smith, J.M. Powis. 1923. *The Moral Life of the Hebrews*. Chicago: University of Chicago.

Smith, Jonathan Z. 1987. "The Domestication of Sacrifice." In *Violent Origins*. Ed. Robert G. Hammerton-Kelly. 149–76.

Smith, Morton. 1975. "A Note on Burning Babies." *JAOS* 95 477–79.

———. 1987. *Palestian Parties and Politics that Shaped the Old Testament*. London: SCM. (First published in 1971.)

Spiegel, Shalom. 1967. *The Last Trial*. Trans. with introduction by Judah Goldin. New York: Schocken.

Stager, Laurence E. and Samuel R. Wolff. 1984. "Child Sacrifice at Carthage. Religious Rite or Population Control?" *BAR* 10:31–51.

Stern, Philip D. 1989. "A Window on Ancient Israel's Religious Experience: The Herem Re-investigated and Re-interpreted." Unpublished Ph.D. Diss. New York University.

———. 1991. *The Biblical Herem. A Window on Israel's Religious Experience*. Brown Judaic Studies 211. Atlanta: Scholars Press.

Stieglecker, Hermann. 1950a. "Harte und Grausamkeit im Alten Testament." *Theologische Praktische Quartalschrift* 2:9–30.

———. 1950b. "Harte und Grausamkeit im Alten Testament." *Theologische Praktische Quartalschrift* 2:105–28.

Stout, Jeffrey. 1990. "Justice and Resort to War: A Sampling of Christian Ethical Thinking." In James Johnson Turner and John Kelsay, eds. *Cross, Crescent, and Sword.* 3–33.

Stulman, Louis. 1990. "Encroachment in Deuteronomy: An Analysis of the Social World of the D Code." *JBL* 109:613–32.

Toombs, L.E. 1962. "War, Ideas of." *IDB.* Vol. 4:787–98.

van Oyen, Hendrik. 1967. *Ethik des Alten Testaments.* Gütersloh: Gerd Mohn.

Vayda, Andrew P. 1967. "Hypotheses about Functions of War." In Morton Fried, Marvin Harris, and Robert Murphy, eds. *War: The Anthropology of Armed Conflict and Aggression.* 85–92.

———. 1968. "Primitive War." In Leon Bramson and George W. Goethals, eds. *War.* 275–82.

———. 1976. *War in Ecological Perspectives: Persistence, Change and Adaptive Processes in Three Oceanian Societies.* New York: Plenum.

Vermeule, Emily. 1979. *Aspects of Death in Early Greek Art and Poetry.* Berkeley: University of California.

von Rad, Gerhard. 1953. *Studies in Deuteronomy.* London: SCM.

———. 1991. *Holy War in Ancient Israel.* Marva J. Dawn and John Howard Yoder, trans. and eds. Grand Rapids, MI: Eerdmans. (Originally published in German in 1958.)

Wager, Günter. 1940. "The Political Organization of the Bantu of Kavirondo." In M. Fortes and E.E. Evans-Pritchard, eds. *African Political Systems.* 197–236.

Wallace, Anthony F.C. 1956. "Revitalization Movements: Some Theoretical Considerations for Their Comparative Study." *American Anthropologist* 58:264–81.

———. 1967. "Psychological Preparations for War." In Morton Fried, Marvin Harris, and Robert Murphy, eds. *War: The Anthropology of Armed Conflict and Aggression.* 173–82.

Walsh, Maurice N. and Barbara G. Scandalis. 1975. "Institutionalized Forms of International Male Aggression." In M.A. Nettleship, R. Dalegivens, and Anderson Nettleship, eds. *War, Its Causes and Correlates.* 135–53.

Walters, LeRoy. 1973. "The Just War and the Crusade: Antitheses or Analogies?" *The Monist* 57/4:584–94.

Walzer, Michael 1977. *Just and Unjust Wars. A Moral Argument With Historical Illustrations.* New York: Basic.

Weinfeld, Moshe. 1972. *Deuteronomy and the Deuteronomic School.* Oxford: Clarendon.

———. 1978. "Burning Babies in Ancient Israel. A Rejoinder to Morton Smith's Article in *JAOS* 95 (1975), pp. 477–479." *UF* 10:411–13.

Weippert, M. 1972. "'Heiliger Krieg' in Israel und Assyrien. Kritische Anmerkungen zu Gerhard von Rads Konzept des 'Heiligen Krieges im alten Israel'." *ZAW* 84:469–93.

Weisengoff, J.P. 1960. "Review of C.H.W. Brekelmans, *De ḥerem.*" *CBQ* 22:443–44.

Wenham, Gordon J. 1981. *Numbers. An Introduction and Commentary.* Downers Grove, IL: Inter-Varsity Press.

West, James King. 1981. *Introduction to the Old Testament.* New York: Macmillan.

Westermann, Claus. 1982. *Elements of Old Testament Theology.* Atlanta: John Knox.

———. 1984/85/86. *Genesis. A Commentary.* 3 Vols. Minneapolis, MN: Augsburg.

Wilson, Edward O. 1978. *On Human Nature.* Cambridge, MA: Harvard University Press.

Wilson, Robert R. 1990. "Ethics in Conflict: Sociological Aspects of Ancient Israelite Ethics." In Susan Niditch, ed. *Text and Tradition.* Semeia Studies. Atlanta, GA: Scholars. 193–205.

Wolff, Hans Walter. 1974. *Anthropology of the Old Testament.* Philadelphia: Fortress.

———. 1977. *Joel and Amos. A Commentary on the Books of the Prophets Joel and Amos.* Philadelphia: Fortress.

Wright, David P. 1985. "Purification from Corpse-Contamination in Numbers XXXI 18–24." *VT* 35:213–23.

Wright, G. Ernst. 1953. *The Book of Deuteronomy. Introduction and Exegesis. IB.* Nashville, TN: Abingdon.

———. 1969. *The Old Testament and Theology.* New York: Harper and Row.

Wright, Quincy. 1942. *A Study of War.* Vols. 1 and 2. Chicago: University of Chicago.

Yadin, Yigael. 1963. *The Art of Warfare in Biblical Lands.* New York: McGraw Hill.

Zakovitch, Yair. 1981. "Siseras Tod." *ZAW* 93:364–74.

Zimmerli, Walther. 1976. *The Old Testament and the World.* Atlanta: John Knox.

ADDITIONAL READINGS

Benedict, Marion J. 1927. *The God of the Old Testament in Relation to War.* New York: Columbia University.

Brekelmans, C.H.W. 1971. "ḥerem, Bann." In E. Jenni and C. Westermann, eds. *Theologische Handworterbuch zum Alten Testament I.* Munich: C. Kaiser 635–39.

Chaney, M. 1983. "Ancient Palestinian Peasant Movements and the Formation of Premonarchic Israel." In D.N. Freedman and D.F. Graff, eds. *Palestine in Transition.* 39–90.

Christensen, Duane L. 1975. *The Transformation of the War Oracle in Old Testament Prophecy.* Missoula: Scholars.

Cooper, Helen M., Adrienne Auslander Munich, and Susan Merrill Squier. 1989. *Arms and the Woman. War, Gender, and Literary Representation.* Chapel Hill, NC: University of North Carolina.

Craigie, Peter C. 1986. "War, Religion and Scripture." *Bulletin of the Canadian Society of Biblical Studies.* 46:3–13.

Cross, Frank Moore. 1973. *Canaanite Myth and Hebrew Epic.* Cambridge, MA: Harvard.

Durbin, E.F.M. and John Bowley. 1939. *Personal Aggressiveness and War.* New York: Columbia University.

Edelman, Diane. 1986. "Saul's Battle Against Ameleq (1 Sam 15)." *JSOT* 35:71–84.

Elshtain, Jean Bethke. 1987. *Women and War.* New York: Basic.

Emerton, J.A. 1971a. "Some False Clues in the Study of Genesis XIV." *VT* 21:24–47.

Enz, J.J. 1972. *The Christian Warfare: The Roots of Pacificism in the Old Testament.* Scottsdale, PA: Herald Press.

Falk, Richard and Samuel Kim. 1980. *The War System: An Interdisciplinary Approach.* Boulder, CO: Westview Press.

Friedman, Richard E. 1981. *The Exile and Biblical Narrative. The Formation of the Deuteronomistic and Priestly Works.* HSM 22. Chico, CA: Scholars.

171

Holmes, Arthur F., ed. 1975. *War and Christian Ethics.* Grand Rapids, MI: Eerdmans.

Huber, Peter Birkett. 1975. "Defending the Cosmos: Violence and Social Order Among the Anggor New Guinea. " In M.A. Nettleship, R. Dalegivens, and Anderson Nettleship, eds. *War, Its Causes and Correlates.* 619–60.

Lind, Millard C. 1971. "Paradigm of Holy War in the Old Testament." *Biblical Research* 16:16–31.

Malamat, Abraham. 1979. "The Israelite Conduct of War in the Israelite Conquest of Canaan." In *Symposium: Celebrating the Seventy-Fifth Anniversary of the American School of Oriental Research (1900–1975).* Philadelphia: ASOR. 35–56.

May, H.G. 1974. "Aspects of the Imagery of World Domination and World State in the Old Testament." In James L. Crenshaw and John T. Willis, eds. *Essays in Old Testament Ethics.* 59–71.

Muilenburg, James. 1961. *The Way of Israel: Biblical Faith and Ethics.* New York: Harper.

Otterbein, Keith. 1973. "The Anthropology of War." In J. Honigmann, ed. *Handbook of Social and Cultural Anthropology.* Chicago: Rand McNally. 923–58.

Ramsey, Paul. 1968. *The Just War. Force and Political Responsibility.* Lanham, Md./New York/London: University Press of America.

Turney-High, Harry Holbert. 1949. *Primitive War.* Columbia, S.C.: University of South Carolina.

INDEX OF BIBLICAL CITATIONS

173

GENERAL INDEX

/7/A